TAMING THE
WILD MUSHROOM

*The discovery of a new dish
does more for human happiness
than the discovery of a new star.*

—ANTHELME BRILLAT-SAVARIN
1825

TAMING THE WILD MUSHROOM

A Culinary Guide to Market Foraging

BY ARLEEN RAINIS BESSETTE AND ALAN E. BESSETTE

UNIVERSITY OF TEXAS PRESS  **AUSTIN**

Frontispiece:
Some mushrooms commonly found in
the marketplace.

LIBRARY OF CONGRESS CATALOGING-IN-PUBLICATION DATA

Bessette, Arleen Rainis, date
    Taming the wild mushroom : a culinary guide to market foraging /
by Arleen Rainis Bessette and Alan E. Bessette.—1st ed.
        p.   cm.
Includes bibliographical references (p.   ) and index.
ISBN 0-292-70798-3 (alk. paper).—ISBN 0-292-70799-1 (pbk. :
alk. paper)
    1. Cookery (Mushrooms)   2. Mushrooms, Edible.   I. Bessette, Alan.
II. Title.
TX804.B35 1993
641.6′58—dc20   92-32991

All photographs are
by Alan E. Bessette and
Arleen Rainis Bessette except
where indicated with initials
at bottom of the photograph
or beside caption.

DA   David Arora
BB   Bill Bakaitis
GM   Gourmet Mushrooms, Inc.
PS   Paul Stamets
JW   James Worrall

Contents

The Recipes

Main Courses

MEAT

Aunt Ruth's Lamb and Mushroom Curry   71
Grilled Flank Steak with White Matsutake   84
Stir-fry Beef with Enokitake Mushrooms   79
Stuffed Pork Chops with Orange-Pineapple Glaze   45
Veal Scaloppine with Mushrooms   20

POULTRY

Baked Chicken with Mushrooms and White Wine–Mustard Sauce   25
Mushroom- and Herb-stuffed Chicken Rolls with Cranberry Glaze   78
Oriental Chicken and Pasta   65
Roast Duckling with Mushroom Dressing and Apple Cider Gravy   43
Turkey-Mushroom Casserole   98

FISH AND SHELLFISH

Baked Fish Fillets with Enokitake   76
Baked Salmon with Crab and Mushroom Stuffing   96
Baked Tuna with White Matsutake and Honey-Mustard Sauce   83
Creamy Seafood Casserole   21
Garlic Shrimp with Mushrooms   59
Grilled Trout Stuffed with Morels and Spring Greens   49
Scallops and White Matsutake with Fennel   86
Seasoned Steamed Clams and Mushrooms   72

PASTA

Manicotti with Tomato and Mushroom Sauce   16
Mushroom Scampi   97
Pasta with Mushroom and Artichoke Sauce   29
Pesto and Mushroom Lasagna   53
Vegetable Fusilli with Cheese Sauce   99

EGGS AND CHEESE

Black Truffle and Cheese Omelet   90
Mushroom and Ham Cheesecake   52
Oyster Mushroom and Sausage Bake   36
Shiitake Frittata   73

TO OUR MOTHERS,
BUNNY RAINIS
AND GLORIA BESSETTE,
WITH LOVE.

THEIR JOYFUL CREATIVITY
IN THE KITCHEN
TAUGHT US
TO TRUST OUR OWN.

Preface

MANY PEOPLE enjoy mushrooms, but few identify, collect, and prepare them for the table. Many are fearful about eating wild mushrooms because of the danger of being poisoned. Over the past several years, a steadily increasing number of cultivated and wild species have been introduced into the marketplace and are now available in most grocery stores, supermarkets, and fresh markets (farmers' markets, produce markets, health food stores). At last it is possible to safely foray for a variety of mushrooms by simply shopping at your local food market.

Taming the Wild Mushroom: A Culinary Guide to Market Foraging is an illustrated sourcebook for identifying and preparing the dozen most commonly available cultivated and wild mushroom species sold in the marketplace. It is not intended as a field guide for identifying and picking wild mushrooms. We wrote it to enhance consumer awareness of the mushroom species available and to provide useful information about their selection, preservation, and preparation. We offer more than fifty recipes.

The design is simple: color photographs and a description introduce and illustrate each species. We tell you how the mushrooms are sold, advise you about their market availability, describe such culinary characteristics as texture and taste, and supply some historical comments. At the end of each section, we present several original recipes. Overall, we hope this book gives you many hours of enjoyment and discovery.

Acknowledgments

THIS BOOK includes contributions by many people besides the authors. Several individuals contributed photographs: we thank David Arora, Bill Bakaitis, Malcolm Clark, Paul Stamets, and Dr. James Worrall. Ruth Rainis and Malcolm Clark each submitted recipes included in this book. We are grateful to Joseph Messina, who provided a variety of mushrooms for photographs and recipes. Permission to include the North American Mycological Association list of known mycological clubs in North America was granted by Dr. Kenneth W. Cochran, the association's executive secretary. We are most appreciative of the many hours of technical assistance provided by Debbie Paciello. Steve Trudell, Sally Groupman, and David Arora deserve special thanks for providing fresh mushrooms, shipped across country, for use in several recipes. We greatly appreciate the efforts and contributions of Bunny Rainis, Joseph Messina and Dr. Paul F. Lehmann, who reviewed the manuscript and made valuable comments and suggestions for its improvement. Our appreciation goes to the entire staff of the University of Texas Press, whose talent and expertise produce finely crafted and beautiful books.

Preceding pages:
A basket of beautiful cultivated and wild mushrooms. Courtesy of Gourmet Mushrooms, Inc.

Opposite:
Dryad's Saddles will not typically be found in the market, but they are common in the spring and can be found on deciduous stumps, often in great quantities.

1.

Introduction

THERE IS A BIT OF MAGIC on the grocer's shelves. People have searched for it for thousands of years. In times of war and extreme need, the mushroom has sustained them. It served as, and still is, a key component in some religious rituals. Valued for its healing powers, it is claimed by some to prolong life, enhance sexual prowess, and cure cancer. More commonly and perhaps most important, it adds complexity and excitement to otherwise ordinary meals. Described as the offspring of the male lightning bolt striking the female earth, the mushroom has emerged from the quiet wood and entered the bustling marketplace.

Often regarded with awe, shrouded in mystery, mistrusted and feared, mushrooms have been neglected and overlooked as a source of variety in the North American culinary tradition. However, in the last decade awareness and appreciation for this fruit of the earth have increased. Mushrooms now show up in unexpected places: next to cellophane-wrapped heads of lettuce, beside green beans—nestled near fresh produce of every kind. No longer limited to white and buff-colored buttons, they come as golden trumpets and creamy pleated shells, as great earth-brown umbrellas and honey-toned sponges. Fresh or dried, pickled, canned, and even frozen in butter sauce with baby spring peas, mushrooms have met us on our own ground to remind us of our neglect and to invite us to rediscover them.

A rediscovery it truly is, for the love of mushrooms goes back to the ancient Greeks, to the ancient Chinese and Japanese, to Aztec and early native American cultures. Mushroom cultivation dates back two thousand or more years in China, to the seventeenth century in France, and to the late 1800s in the United States. Mushrooms were so esteemed by the Romans that pots, called *boleteria,* were specially designed and reserved for their cooking. Trained slaves were the only individuals entrusted with their preparation. You could even determine your own social status by how many and varied were the mushroom dishes served you if you were lucky enough to dine with Roman nobility. Only nobility were allowed access to mushrooms, the common folk being forbidden to pick or consume them.

However, we are talking about more than flavor. From the nutritional standpoint, certain mushroom species have a higher protein content than most vegetables, including legumes. They are low in fat and contain significant amounts of vitamins. Medically, there are research results suggesting that components of some species may reduce serum cholesterol, inhibit tumor growth, stimulate interferon production, or possess antiviral properties.

Now that cultural boundaries between countries are dissolving, international foods are flourishing in the United States. The once exotic has become accepted as expected: culinary traditions of the Orient and the Middle East, of Mexico and Europe, are commonly rep-

Opposite:
Fresh Chanterelles on display at Pike Place Market, Seattle.

resented in our markets and in our homes. It seems only fitting that mushrooms, so highly prized by so many of these cultures, be reintroduced.

Improved technology has eliminated seasonal dependence: mushrooms can be found in one form or another year-round in the marketplace. Increased knowledge about cultivation has allowed easy access to some mushroom varieties that were formerly found only in the wild. Sophisticated packaging and transport have enabled more wild varieties to be available to the consumer. No longer is it necessary to search wood and field for such treasures as King Boletes and Oyster mushrooms, for Shiitake and Chanterelles. They are there on the shelves. Take up your basket. Join us in gathering the magic.

Examples of the many varieties of canned and packaged mushrooms.

2.

Selecting, Preserving, and Cooking Mushrooms

What Are Mushrooms?

Mushrooms are one example of a very large and diverse group of organisms called *fungi*. They are similar to plants, but lack chlorophyll and cannot produce their own food through the process of photosynthesis. They are decomposers and obtain food by absorbing nutrients from materials such as decaying wood, leaves, compost, and soil. They are classified in the Kingdom Fungi.

Mushrooms are known as fleshy fungi because they are fruiting bodies. Like apples that bear seeds, mushrooms produce microscopic seeds called *spores*. The remainder of the fungus is called the *mycelium*. It consists of a mass of entangled microscopic filaments that permeate the decomposing material. Some mushroom species fruit at only one time during the year, and they will only be available in the market during their fruiting season.

The typical mushroom has a cap, stem, and thin bladelike spore-producing structures called *gills* that are on the underside of the cap. However, some mushroom species do not have gills. Instead, the underside of the cap will be spongelike with tiny pores. Still others are irregularly shaped and lack a cap, stem, gills, or pores.

While some variation occurs from species to species, the composition and nutritional value of edible mushrooms is remarkably similar. Most mushrooms contain approximately 90 percent water. They have few calories, usually only fifteen to forty-five per quarter pound. Their fat and carbohydrate content is negligible, and they contain no cholesterol. They are a rich source of protein. Many mushrooms contain vitamins B, C, and D, and a few also have vitamin A; however, some vitamins may be destroyed during the cooking process. Several minerals, such as phosphates and potassium salts, are also found in mushrooms. Although mushrooms by themselves are not a complete source of nutrition, when combined with other foods they contribute significantly to a well-balanced diet.

Selecting and Preserving Mushrooms

As with any other fresh produce you might buy, select only those mushrooms that are firm and fresh. Signs of decay are soft or mushy spots, areas that are discolored, dried and woody edges of caps, a slimy and/or sticky surface, and an obviously disagreeable odor. While cultivated species are generally insect free, wild species should be checked for infestation. Look for holes at the base of the stem, and feel the stem to see if it is firm. A hollow or soft and yielding stem may indicate that it is riddled with the tunnels of larvae or adult insects. Many cases of so-called mushroom poisoning are the result of eating spoiled or decayed mushrooms or those infested by insects. When cleaning mushrooms, remember that most of their flavor is located in their "skin"; therefore, use water sparingly, if at all. Wipe

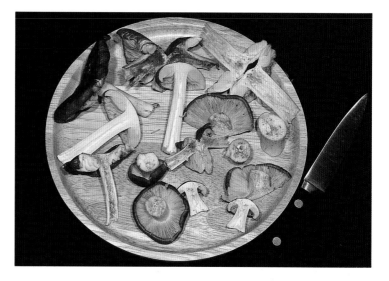

Sectioned mushrooms showing larval infestation and spoilage. Note larvae, larval holes, and discoloration.

debris gently from their surface using a soft brush or a damp paper towel or cloth. Brushes made specifically for cleaning mushrooms can be purchased in culinary specialty shops. Use a small sharp knife for any trimming that might be needed.

Below are six techniques you can use to store or preserve mushrooms.

REFRIGERATION: Store uncleaned mushrooms in paper bags, in waxed paper, or in their original containers. Do not store them in plastic wrap, plastic bags, or airtight plastic containers. They all retain moisture and hasten decay. Once refrigerated, mushrooms will keep for about a week. Clean them just prior to use.

FREEZING: This is a simple technique that allows mushrooms to be kept for up to a year. There are several ways to freeze them, depending both on the type of mushroom and the amount you have. Some are best frozen after sautéing for two to three minutes in butter. You may also blanch mushrooms for two to three minutes in water that has a teaspoon of lemon juice or white vinegar added to it, or steam mushrooms for three to four minutes before freezing. Slicing and cooking them for one to two minutes on High in a microwave oven also works well. Regardless of the technique you use, always cool mushrooms before placing them in freezer bags or containers. You can also freeze some mushrooms raw. Clean them and dip them into a solution of lemon juice or white vinegar and water (about 1 teaspoon per gallon of water), dry with paper towels, separate on a cookie sheet or baking pan, and freeze. Once the mushrooms are frozen, remove them from the pan and store them in plastic bags or freezer containers. When using frozen mushrooms, add them directly without thawing. This helps maintain their shape and texture.

DRYING: This is perhaps the oldest preservation technique and the most simple. Clean the mushrooms, slice or halve them (depending on their size), and place them in a commercial dehydrator on medium-low heat for twenty-four hours. Dehydrators may be purchased in culinary specialty shops and health food stores or from sources advertised in mushroom journals. If you do not have a dehydrator, you can dry mushrooms in the oven of a gas stove by the heat of the pilot flame (with the oven door partially open), on screens or racks over a wood stove, in a protected and dry area in the sun, or by stringing the mushrooms on thread and hanging them in a dry and well-ventilated area. Once they are thoroughly dry, place them for a day or two in closed paper bags to remove any last bits of moisture. Then store them in airtight jars or containers. Dried mushrooms will keep indefinitely. Their flavor is concentrated and enhanced by drying, and improves with age.

Typical food dehydrator for drying mushrooms.

CANNING: This technique retains more of the flavor and texture of fresh mushrooms than any other method. Always use a pressure canner. **Never can mushrooms using a hot water bath method because of the risk of botulism with improperly canned mushrooms.** Clean and trim mushrooms. Soak in cold water for ten minutes. Drain. Rinse under running water. Cut large mushrooms in halves or quarters. Leave small mushrooms whole. For raw pack: Place mushrooms into clean canning jars, leaving one-half-inch head space. Add one-fourth teaspoon salt to half pints, and one-half tea-

Dried Morels.

spoon salt to pints. Cover with boiling water, adjust lids, and process at ten pounds pressure for thirty minutes. For hot pack: Steam mushrooms for four minutes, or simmer gently in a covered pan without adding any liquid for about fifteen minutes. Pack in clean, hot jars, leaving one-half-inch head space. Add the same amount of salt as above, and add mushroom liquid from steaming or cooking, using additional boiling water as needed. Adjust lids and process at fifteen pounds pressure for twenty minutes.

SALTING: A very old technique, salting is traditional in Russia and Baltic countries. Clean and trim mushrooms. Layer them in a glass or ceramic jar or crock, sprinkling the layers with rock, sea, or pickling salt. Use about two tablespoons of salt per pound of mushrooms. Cover the mushrooms, and weight the lid using a stone, brick, or other heavy object. Store in the refrigerator or other cool location. The mushrooms will release their juices and flatten, allowing you to add more layers as desired. They are ready for consumption after three days. They can be eaten raw or used in cooking. Rinsing is optional.

PICKLED OR MARINATED MUSHROOMS: Best used in salads or as appetizers and hors d'oeuvres, mushrooms preserved in pickling solution or marinade are delicious. This simple method consists of simmering mushrooms for five to ten minutes and then storing them in an acidic marinade or pickling solution. Always clean and trim mushrooms carefully. Slice or chop large mushrooms into bite-size pieces.

Pickled mushrooms.

Keep small mushrooms and buttons whole. Always store in clean, airtight, noncorrosive containers. See the recipe section for instructions for preparing specific simmering solutions, marinades, and pickling solutions.

Cooking with Mushrooms

When cooking with mushrooms, consider their texture and flavor. Texture will vary among mushroom types, some species being crisp, others chewy, and still others smooth and buttery. There are also differences in texture among the different parts of a single mushroom. For example, the cap may be tender and the stem tough or inedible. Flavors will also differ widely among even the dozen mushrooms presented in this book. This difference is most noticeable once the mushrooms are cooked. It is useful to become familiar with a mushroom's signature taste to best complement it in your cooking. When tasting a mushroom for the first time, sauté a bit of it in some butter and taste it. This is the best way to experience its particular culinary characteristics and will enable you to use it more creatively in your cooking. Helpful cooking hints are presented with each mushroom description. As with any new food, mushroom species being eaten for the first time should be tried in small portions. Just as some people are allergic to common foods such as wheat, milk, or peanut butter, so a few individuals may react negatively to particular types of mushrooms. Such responses may be characterized by gastro-

Preparing mushrooms for cooking.

intestinal upset—nausea, vomiting, and diarrhea—or by such mild skin reactions as hives.

Standard ingredients used in mushroom preparation include butter (not margarine), onion and its relatives (leeks, green onions, shallots), garlic, sweet peppers, nuts, dried fruits, such wines as Madeira and sherry, and a multitude of herbs and spices. Olive oil is also used, especially for sautéing King Boletes and for pickling and marinating. Using fresh herbs and spices, rather than dried or powdered ones, produces superior results. We have provided a chart of equivalents and substitutions, as well as metric conversion charts, to assist you in choosing ingredients (see page 107).

Fresh mushrooms consist of approximately 90 percent water. Expect them to lose from 20 percent to 40 percent of their volume once they are cooked. To determine the amount to buy or cook, refer to the equivalents and substitutions chart. It is usual to plan on four ounces of fresh mushrooms per person; however, we (as well as most of our friends) have been known to eat greater amounts! Since fresh mushrooms of your choice may not always be available, canned or dried varieties may be substituted in most of the recipes presented in this book.

Be creative! Experiment with mushroom choices listed at the end of each recipe. Try mixing mushroom species or combining portions of reconstituted dried mushrooms with canned and/or fresh. Most dried mushrooms can be ground into powder using a mortar and pestle. Dried Shiitake mushrooms are one exception, inasmuch as they are too leatherlike to grind easily. Mushroom powder can be

A variety of mushroom powders.

stored indefinitely in airtight containers. Use it in making gravies, sauces, and soups; sprinkle it over fish or poultry prior to baking; add it to grains or pasta; or incorporate it into butter and cheese spreads.

A number of cooking methods are used in the recipes in this book. Cooking times and temperatures are approximate because of the variable water content of mushrooms. It is always a good idea to check periodically throughout the cooking process to decide if more or less heat or time is required. Six common mushroom cooking methods are described below.

Sautéing mushrooms.

SAUTÉING: Depending on the results you prefer, you may choose any of three sautéing methods. One is to cook the mushrooms on high heat, in oil or in a combination of oil and butter, for approximately two minutes. Butter alone is not used because it will burn with high heat. You may use clarified butter, or use oil and add butter at the end of cooking. This high-heat sauté reduces the amount of water loss from the mushroom. The result is mushrooms at maximum volume that are crisp and mild.

The second technique is to sauté the mushrooms in butter over low-medium heat for approximately fifteen minutes or until all the mushrooms' liquid has been released and has evaporated. This longer, slower cooking results in softer mushrooms of less volume with a more concentrated and intense flavor.

The third sautéing method is a variation on the second. The mushrooms are cooked in butter over low heat until the mushrooms' liquid has been released; however, do not allow it to evaporate. Rather, add to it a touch of mild stock or some wine. Continue cooking until it thickens; season to taste, and you have a lovely sauce in which your mushrooms may swim. When sautéing mushrooms, you can achieve a blend of flavors by combining onions and/or garlic during the cooking. Add additional spices toward the end.

FRYING: This might be considered still another variation of sautéing. But with this method, mushrooms are dipped in batter, dredged in flour (or coated in bread crumbs or other dry mixtures), and then cooked over relatively high heat in oil or oil and butter combinations. The oil and coating work together to retain the fluid inside the mushroom. The final result should be a mushroom crisp on the outside and deliciously juicy on the inside.

BROILING: Certain mushrooms lend themselves excellently to broiling because of their sturdy texture and/or cap size. Some of these are the White Button, the Shiitake, and the Wine-cap Stropharia. Here is the chance to work creative magic with stuffings, toppings, and spices. Because of mushrooms' high water content, they can be cooked until heated through without any real risk of burning. Occasionally the edges may brown too rapidly. Prevent this by moving them farther from the heat source. Initially, start broiling mushrooms as close to the source of heat as possible. Move them if necessary.

GRILLING: The same rules apply for grilling as for broiling. The only real difference is that the heat source is now under the mushrooms instead of over them. We enjoy marinating and/or basting the mushrooms with savory sauces when grilling or broiling them.

BAKING: Those same sturdy mushrooms that do so well when broiled or grilled, bake wonderfully. Either fill or stuff them, or embed them in savory matrixes subtly spiced. Using baking pans of different shapes (muffin or bread) or puff pastry dough and filo adds visual, textural, and taste complexity.

BLANCHING: This technique, discussed in Chapter 2, is also a useful cooking technique for preparing mushrooms for use in soups and sauces. For a change of taste, try blanching your mushrooms in a variety of liquids, from stocks to wines. The liquid resulting from blanching may be suitable for use as a consommé. Add a bit of salt and taste it. If the flavor is appealing, add additional spices as desired; if not, discard it.

Opposite:
A bit of magic on the grocery shelves: a mushroom display at Edwards Food Superstore, Shrewsbury, Mass.

The following represent the dozen most common mushrooms found in the marketplace. They may be found in supermarkets, shops specializing in fresh produce, farmers' markets, health food stores, and Oriental markets. See page 103 for information regarding specialty food suppliers that sell mushrooms.

3.

Mushrooms in the Marketplace

White Button
Agaricus brunnescens

OTHER NAMES: *Agaricus bisporus,* Common Store Mushroom, Commercial Mushroom, Button Mushroom, Market Mushroom, Cream Mushroom.

DESCRIPTION: The cap at button stage is 1–3 inches wide and umbrella shaped with an inrolled edge. Color—white, cream, or pale brown—varies with the variety. The surface is typically smooth and dry but may have tiny flattened scales. The stem is short and thick and is attached to the center of the cap. It is white to pale brown and supports a narrow band of white tissue at the top that covers the gills. The undersurface of the cap has gills, whose color varies with maturity. In a very young button, the gills are pink. As the button matures, gills become reddish brown and, finally, chocolate brown. The cap and stem flesh is thick, firm, and white. The White Button is easily cultivated on enriched wheat straw or rye grain.

HOW SOLD: Fresh, dried, canned, pickled, or frozen.

MARKET AVAILABILITY: Year-round.

CULINARY ASPECTS: Cultivated.

The White Button is the most commonly cultivated, consumed, and recognized mushroom in this country. It is one of the three most commonly cultivated mushrooms worldwide. When most people think of mushrooms, this is the mushroom that comes to mind. Because of this, the White Button is often used as the standard against which other mushrooms, cultivated and wild, are compared. Both cap and stem are edible. The flavor is described as meaty, mushroomy, and earthy. Its texture is firm, with a silky aspect when cooked. The White Button can be eaten raw or cooked and can be used in any recipe calling for mushrooms. It can be prepared using almost any cooking method. Young, unopened buttons have the best flavor. Old, mature mushrooms have a much stronger flavor and will spoil more quickly. When cooked, they shrink somewhat and release a good bit of liquid, requiring that cooks take shrinkage into account in determining how many to prepare.

The best way to clean the White Button is to use a mushroom brush. Clean these mushrooms, as others, without water if at all possible. If you must use water, allow the mushrooms to drain on paper toweling for 10–15 minutes prior to cooking.

This mushroom can be preserved by drying, canning, pickling, or sautéing followed by freezing. Uncleaned, fresh mushrooms will keep well in the refrigerator for up to a week if stored in paper bags or waxed paper.

COMMENTS: The White Button is known to have been cultivated in France in the 1700s, where it was called *Champignon*. Originally

Opposite:
Fresh White Buttons.

Dried White Buttons.

brown, a white variety appeared in a farmer's field in Pennsylvania in 1926. Strains from this variant were cultivated and have given us to-day's common domesticated mushroom. With the increased interest in mushroom consumption, a variety of *Agaricus* species are now available in the marketplace. Creminis (*Agaricus cupreobrunneus*) are typically darker brown and have firmer flesh, and Portobellos have larger caps and resemble umbrellas. All can be used interchangeably in cooking.

Chinese research has found that the White Button contains enzymes that may improve digestion and lower blood pressure. Other substances similar to those found in Shiitake mushrooms that are known to lower blood cholesterol are also present in this mushroom.

Baked Mushrooms and Winter Vegetables

Preheat oven to 350°F.

Combine all ingredients, except mushrooms, in a baking dish. Bake uncovered for 30 minutes. Add mushrooms, mixing briefly. Continue baking another 30–40 minutes or until vegetables are tender without being mushy.

Serves 4.

Other mushroom choices: Shiitake, Wine-cap Stropharia, White Matsutake, Paddy Straw.

2 cups peeled and cubed butternut squash (1-inch cubes)
1 cup cubed red potatoes (1-inch cubes)
1 cup parsnips (1-inch rounds)
4 cloves garlic, minced
¼ cup minced fresh parsley
¼ cup olive oil
1 teaspoon salt
⅛ teaspoon freshly ground black pepper
6 large White Button mushrooms (about 2½-inch caps), quartered

Manicotti with Tomato and Mushroom Sauce

8–10 ounces White Button
  mushrooms, sliced ½-inch
  thick
1 cup coarsely chopped onion
4 cloves garlic, minced
3 tablespoons olive oil
1 29-ounce can tomato sauce
½ teaspoon each thyme and
  rosemary
1 teaspoon each oregano and
  basil
¼ cup minced fresh parsley

2 teaspoons sugar
½ teaspoon salt
¼ teaspoon crushed red pepper
  flakes
½ cup whole pitted medium
  black olives
12 manicotti shells, cooked
  until barely tender (about 5
  minutes) and stuffed with
  your favorite filling

Sauté mushrooms, onions, and garlic in olive oil over medium-high heat for 5 minutes. Combine with all remaining ingredients (except stuffed shells) and simmer for 30 minutes.

Preheat oven to 350°F.

Place stuffed shells in a baking dish. Cover with sauce. Cover with aluminum foil and bake for 30 minutes.

Serves 4 to 6.

Other mushroom choices: Shiitake, Wine-cap Stropharia.

Snail-stuffed Mushrooms

Preheat oven to 375°F.

Sauté shallots and garlic in butter until translucent. Whisk in flour and cook 3 minutes over medium heat. Whisk in bouillon and half and half, cooking until thickened. Stir in lemon juice. Sauce will be quite thick.

Remove stems from mushrooms; save for other recipes. Brush caps with vegetable oil and place gill side up on an ungreased baking sheet. Place one small snail, or half a large snail, in each cap. Place a dollop of sauce on top. Bake at 375°F for 10 minutes, barely browning the edges of the sauce. Garnish with minced fresh parsley.

Makes 1 dozen.

Other mushroom choices: Shiitake, Wine-cap Stropharia.

2 teaspoons minced shallots
1 clove garlic, minced
3 tablespoons butter
2 tablespoons flour
¼ cup bouillon (vegetable or chicken)
¼ cup half and half
¼ teaspoon lemon juice
12 large (2- to 3-inch caps) White Button mushrooms
Vegetable oil
12 small snails or 6 large snails, halved; or smoked baby clams; or oysters
Fresh parsley for garnish

Stuffed Mushroom Caps

12 large (2- to 3-inch caps)
  White Button mushrooms
2 slices bacon
2 scallions with tops, finely
  chopped
1 bunch sorrel or watercress,
  chopped (about ½ cup)
½ cup grated Edam cheese
¼ cup bread crumbs
1 tablespoon cooking sherry
¼ teaspoon salt
¼ teaspoon black pepper
Vegetable oil

Preheat oven to 375°F.

Remove stems from mushrooms and chop finely. Fry bacon until crisp; remove from pan. Sauté chopped mushroom stems, scallions, and sorrel in bacon fat until sorrel is wilted. Crumble bacon. Combine all ingredients, including bacon, and mix well.

Brush mushroom caps with oil. Stuff with filling, rounding the tops. Bake on ungreased baking sheet at 375°F for 10 minutes.

Makes 1 dozen.

Other mushroom choices: Shiitake, Wine-cap Stropharia.

Swiss Chard and Mushrooms

Sauté mushrooms in bacon fat for 2 minutes over medium-high heat. Reduce heat to simmer-low. Chop green onions and tops, and add them to mushrooms. Cover and cook 15–20 minutes, mixing occasionally.

While mushrooms are cooking, clean Swiss chard and cut into 2-inch pieces. Put in large saucepan, add an inch of water, and grate garlic over the top. Cover and steam until tender (about 10 minutes).

Add sour cream and horseradish to mushrooms. Mix well. Season with salt and plenty of freshly ground black pepper. Drain Swiss chard, place in serving dishes, and spoon mushroom mixture on top.

Makes two generous servings.

Other mushroom choices: Morel, Wine-cap Stropharia, Oyster, Paddy Straw.

½ **pound White Button mushrooms, sliced ½-inch thick**
1 **tablespoon bacon fat**
4 **green onions**
1 **pound fresh Swiss chard**
1 **large clove garlic**
2 **tablespoons sour cream**
1 **teaspoon horseradish**
Freshly ground black pepper

Veal Scaloppine with Mushrooms

8 ounces White Button
  mushrooms, cut ½-inch thick
3 cloves garlic, minced
½ cup coarsely chopped onion
2 medium bell peppers, coarsely
  chopped
1 tablespoon olive oil
2 teaspoons minced fresh thyme
  (¼ teaspoon dried)
½ cup red wine
1 cup beef stock
¼ teaspoon pepper
1 pound veal scaloppine

In a large skillet, sauté mushrooms, garlic, onion, and peppers in olive oil for about 2 minutes over medium-high heat, stirring constantly. Add thyme, wine, beef stock, and pepper. Add salt to taste. Bring to a boil, and then reduce heat and simmer, uncovered, 5 minutes. Add veal; simmer until cooked through.

Serves 2.

Other mushroom choices: Shiitake, King Bolete, Paddy Straw, Oyster.

Creamy Seafood Casserole

1 cup medium-grain rice
1 egg, beaten
½ cup chopped fresh parsley
½ cup chopped sun-dried
   tomatoes
½ cup butter
1 medium onion, chopped
3 cloves garlic, minced
2 stalks celery, chopped
4 cups (¾ pound) sliced White
   Button mushrooms
¼ cup chopped fresh dill
1 teaspoon each salt and white
   pepper
1 pound uncooked shrimp
1 pound imitation crab meat,
   cut into bite-sized pieces
¼ cup flour
1½ cups milk
1 8-ounce package cream cheese
¼ teaspoon thyme

Topping:

½ cup bread crumbs
¼ cup grated Parmesan cheese

In a 2-quart saucepan, bring rice to a boil in 2 cups water. Reduce to simmer, cover, and cook 15 minutes. Remove from heat; stir in egg, parsley, and tomatoes. Line a buttered 13- × 9-inch baking dish with mixture.

Bring 2 cups water to a gentle simmer; poach shrimp for 3 minutes or until firm and pink. Drain, reserving 1 cup liquid. Shell and devein.

Melt 4 tablespoons butter in a 6-quart pot. Add onion, garlic, and celery; sauté over medium heat 10 minutes, mixing occasionally. Add mushrooms and cook until they release their liquid, about 10 minutes. Add dill, salt, pepper, shrimp, and imitation crab meat. Mix well.

Melt remaining butter in a 2-quart saucepan. Whisk in flour and cook over medium heat, whisking continuously, for 1 minute. Gradually add milk and liquid from shrimp. Cook, mixing often, until thickened. Add cream cheese and thyme, whisking until cream cheese is melted. Stir into seafood mixture, mixing well. Spoon over rice in baking dish.

Preheat oven to 325°F.

Combine bread crumbs and Parmesan cheese. Sprinkle evenly over casserole. Bake for 40–50 minutes, until heated through and golden brown.

Makes 8 servings.

Other mushroom choices: Shiitake, Oyster, Morel.

King Bolete
Boletus edulis

OTHER NAMES: Cep, Porcini, Steinpilz, Penny Bun, Stone Mushroom.

DESCRIPTION: The cap is 2–8 inches wide, is umbrella shaped and incurved when young, and becomes nearly flat with age. It is pale yellowish brown to dark reddish brown, smooth, moist, and firm. The stem is 3–8 inches long, ¾–1¼ inches thick, and solid. It is white to yellowish brown with white to pale brown netlike ridges on its upper portion. Typically, it has an enlarged base. The undersurface of the cap has many tiny pores and is white to dingy yellow. The cap and stem flesh is thick, firm, and white. It grows singly or in groups on the ground under conifers and hardwoods.

HOW SOLD: Fresh and dried.

MARKET AVAILABILITY: Fresh King Boletes are seasonally available, usually September through November. Dried King Boletes are available year-round.

CULINARY ASPECTS: Wild.

The King Bolete is perhaps the most sought-after and prized of all wild mushrooms. Well known to villager and gourmet chefs alike, this mushroom has a flavor that is wonderfully robust and a texture that is sturdy and meaty.

Because of its distinctive and assertive flavor, it can be used with beef and onion dishes without being overwhelmed. It is excellent in soups, sauces, and stuffings and complements strongly flavored fish.

Opposite:
Dried King Boletes and fresh (*left*) as they are found in the North American woods.

One of the easiest and most delicious ways to prepare it is to sauté it in olive oil and to season it with salt and pepper and a light touch of garlic. The essence, or extract, produced by dried King Boletes during reconstitution is close to magical. Use it to make consommé; to initiate a base for sauces, gravies, and soups; or to moisten stuffing mixtures. Supplement other mushroom recipes with the addition of some King Boletes, and you have enhanced an otherwise ordinary dish.

To clean King Boletes, remove debris with a brush. Never peel them or wash them in water. Trim the base of the stem and check for worm holes or larvae. A few will not detract from your recipe; however, make certain that the stem is firm to the touch, never soft. If soft, the stem has more than a few unwelcome inhabitants! If the pores are soggy, you may wish to remove them using a sharp knife. Leave them intact if you are planning to dry the mushrooms.

To reconstitute dried King Boletes, soak them in warm water for approximately 15 minutes. Squeeze all fluid from the mushrooms in order to salvage every last bit of extract. Chop or mince remaining mushrooms and add to soups, gravies, scrambled eggs, casseroles, or other dishes. Dried King Boletes improve with age. It is not unusual to have some of the finest extracts reconstituted from mushrooms that have been stored for two or more years.

Besides drying, canning or salting can preserve King Boletes. Some folks enjoy eating them slivered and raw, but we do not recommend this.

COMMENTS: King Boletes have been enjoyed for centuries. In ancient Rome, they were known as Suilli, which meant *swine*. This is reflected today in the name *porcini,* which is derived from the Italian word for *pig*. Various mushrooms are known to have been used by the Romans to poison aristocrats and to conceal poisons in such assassinations. This may be why mushrooms were sometimes referred to as "food of the gods." King Boletes are so delicious that their heavenly flavor earns them this appellation based on their flavor alone.

Dried King Boletes are very high in protein, surpassing all vegetables except legumes. Studies suggest that extracts made from them may inhibit the growth of a type of cancer called a *sarcoma;* therefore, there could be some truth in the old Eastern European folk belief of the King Bolete's having anticancer properties.

Baked Chicken with Mushrooms and White Wine–Mustard Sauce

Preheat oven to 350°F.

Place chicken, skin side up, in a buttered baking dish. Sprinkle with minced garlic. Cover with sliced mushrooms. Combine mustard, wine, and thyme; pour evenly over mushrooms and chicken. Sprinkle with pepper, cheese, and, lastly, paprika.

Bake, covered, for 30 minutes. Uncover and continue baking an additional 20–30 minutes until juices run clear and top is nicely browned.

Serves 4–6.

Other mushroom choices: White Button, Shiitake, Oyster, Wine-cap Stropharia.

2 pounds chicken, breasts or thighs
2 cloves garlic, minced
6–8 ounces King Boletes, sliced ¼-inch thick
¼ cup Dijon-style mustard
¼ cup dry white wine
1 teaspoon dried thyme
Freshly ground black pepper
¼ cup grated Parmesan cheese
Paprika

Photo shows alternate mushroom choice.

Cream of Asparagus and Mushroom Soup

½ ounce dried King Boletes
1 cup half and half
1 14½-ounce can asparagus
5 green onions, whites only,
  minced
1 large clove garlic, minced
2 tablespoons butter
1 tablespoon flour
1 cup water
2 teaspoons fresh lemon juice
1 teaspoon salt
½ teaspoon white pepper
Roasted sweet red pepper for
  garnish (optional)

Simmer, without boiling, dried mushrooms in half and half for 30 minutes. Puree asparagus, with its liquid, in food processor or blender. Sauté onions and garlic in butter until translucent, being careful not to burn or brown garlic. Add flour and cook 3 minutes, mixing constantly. Whisk in water and cook, stirring constantly, until thickened. Slowly add pureed asparagus, mixing constantly; add lemon juice, salt, and white pepper.

Using a slotted spoon, remove mushrooms from half and half. Puree in a food processor or blender, or mince finely with a sharp knife. Add to asparagus mixture. Slowly add half and half to asparagus mixture, stirring constantly. Heat without boiling. Garnish with bits of roasted sweet red pepper.

Serves 4 as an appetizer, 2 as a main course.

Other mushroom choices: dried Chanterelles, dried Morels.

Cream of Mushroom Soup

In a covered saucepan, sauté carrot, celery, and onion in butter for 30 minutes, mixing occasionally. While vegetables are cooking, add mushrooms, water, salt, sugar, and bouillon granules to a large saucepan, and bring them to a boil. Reduce heat and simmer uncovered 30 minutes.

Drain mushrooms, reserving liquid. Chop mushrooms coarsely. Add flour to vegetables, mixing well. Slowly stir in reserved mushroom liquid. Bring to a boil; reduce heat; and simmer until thickened, mixing constantly. Add chopped mushrooms and parsley to vegetables. Simmer 15 minutes. Stir in half and half and wine. Heat without boiling. Season to taste with salt and pepper.

Serves 4.

Other mushroom choices: dried White Buttons, dried Morels, dried Chanterelles.

1 carrot, minced
1 stalk celery, minced
½ cup minced onion
1 tablespoon butter
2 ounces dried King Boletes
5 cups water
1 teaspoon salt
¼ teaspoon sugar
2 teaspoons beef bouillon
  granules (or 2 cubes)
4 tablespoons flour
¼ cup fresh minced parsley
¾ cup half and half
1 tablespoon dry red wine

Mushroom Mayonnaise Sauce

1 ounce dried King Boletes
½ cup water
1 teaspoon soy sauce
½ cup mayonnaise
¼ cup sour cream
1 tablespoon sun-dried tomato
  paste
¼ teaspoon garlic salt
1 tablespoon minced fresh
  parsley
⅛ teaspoon white pepper

Place mushrooms in a small saucepan with water and soy sauce. Bring to a boil, cover, and turn off heat. Allow to stand 30 minutes or more. Puree mushrooms, along with the liquid, in a blender or food processor. Add remaining ingredients and puree until smooth.

Serve warm over vegetables, poultry, or seafood.

Makes about 1 cup sauce.

Other mushroom choices: dried Shiitake, dried Morels.

Pasta with Mushroom and Artichoke Sauce

Sauté mushrooms and garlic in olive oil over medium heat for 5 minutes; add paprika and continue cooking another 2–3 minutes, mixing often. Add tomatoes and liquid from canned artichoke hearts. Bring to a boil, and then reduce to simmer. Cut artichoke hearts into quarters; add to saucepan. Add all remaining ingredients and salt to taste. Simmer to desired thickness.

Serve over favorite pasta that has been cooked al dente.

Makes about 4 cups of sauce.

Other mushroom choices: White Button, Wine-cap Stropharia, Shiitake.

8 ounces King Boletes, sliced ½-inch thick
2 cloves garlic, minced
3 tablespoons olive oil
1 tablespoon paprika
1 28-ounce can crushed tomatoes
1 8½-ounce can artichoke hearts
¼ cup dry red wine
1 tablespoon grated Parmesan cheese
1–2 pinches of sugar

Photo shows alternate mushroom choice.

Oyster Mushroom

Pleurotus ostreatus complex

OTHER NAMES: Shellfish Mushroom, Abalone.

DESCRIPTION: The cap is 2–8 inches wide and shaped like an oyster shell. It is white to grayish brown and smooth. The stem is ½–1 inch long, and it is attached off center near the cap edge or is absent altogether. It is white to pale yellow and may be coated with tiny yellowish velvety hairs near its base. White gills that descend the stem are found on the undersurface of the cap. The cap and stem flesh is thick, watery, and white. Often the mushroom has a licorice odor. It grows singly or in overlapping clusters on hardwoods, especially poplar, willow, and beech.

HOW SOLD: Fresh, canned, or dried.

MARKET AVAILABILITY: Year-round.

CULINARY CHARACTERISTICS: Cultivated and wild.

The Oyster mushroom is versatile and can be substituted in any recipe calling for the White Button mushroom. Its flavor is mild and sweet, and its texture is fragile and soft. Both the cap and stem are edible. Its odor is mild to absent, except for wild varieties that may have an anise, or licoricelike, odor. Cultivated varieties come in multiple colors: gray, blue, yellow, and even pinks. Think of the visual treats in store when "designing" a recipe utilizing these mushrooms! Particularly good cooking techniques for the Oyster mushroom are stir or deep frying, sautéing, and braising. Some folks enjoy eating them raw in salads, but we do not recommend this. Oyster mushrooms are complemented by onions, butter, mild cheeses, fish, chicken, cream sauces, and gentle herbs.

To clean Oyster mushrooms, trim debris from the lower portion of the stem. If the stems appear tough, discard them. Rinse gills under cold running water, and dry mushrooms between layers of

Opposite:
Fresh Oyster Mushrooms and dried (*above*).

toweling. Because of the fragility of their flesh, Oyster mushrooms should be used as quickly as possible.

To preserve Oyster mushrooms, sauté them in butter and freeze. They may also be dried, though this is not our favorite means of preserving this delicate beauty. Once dried, Oyster mushrooms may be simply added directly to whatever you're cooking without reconstituting.

COMMENTS: The Oyster mushroom is considered a complex because it consists of several closely related species that are so similar they are nearly indistinguishable. While cultivated in China and Japan for decades, until recently it was available in this country only in the wild. Mycological researchers have mastered culturing the Oyster mushroom, and it is now readily available year-round in most marketplaces.

It is not clear if this mushroom was named for its resemblance to oyster shells, or because its flavor is reminiscent of the shellfish. Regardless, it is delicious! A few people have reported experiencing mild gastrointestinal upset, such as indigestion and diarrhea, after eating it. If you have never tried it before, eat a small portion the first time to ensure that you are not one of the unfortunate few who react adversely to it.

Species of the Oyster mushroom complex have been used as fodder for donkeys as well as in Chinese medicine to treat painful tendons, legs, blood vessels, and lumbago.

Oyster Mushrooms for sale at Pike Place Market, Seattle.

Cajun Canapés

Preheat oven to 400°F.

Sauté onions and mushrooms in butter over medium-high heat for 10 minutes, stirring frequently. Add parsley and Tabasco sauce. Place pizza crust on cookie sheet. Spread with grated cheese. Spread mushroom mixture over cheese. Bake for approximately 20 minutes or until edges just begin to brown and center is bubbly. Cut into 2-inch squares.

Makes approximately 24 canapés.

Other mushroom choices: White Button, Wine-cap Stropharia, White Matsutake.

1 cup finely chopped onion
1½ cups finely chopped Oyster mushrooms
¼ cup butter
¼ cup minced fresh parsley
1 teaspoon Tabasco or hot pepper sauce
1 12-inch prepared pizza crust
4 ounces grated mozzarella cheese

Photo shows alternate mushroom choice.

Mushroom Fritters

2 cups finely chopped Oyster
   mushrooms
¼ cup minced bell pepper
2 scallions with tops, minced
2 teaspoons flour
¼ teaspoon salt
Dash cayenne pepper
1 egg, separated
Butter

Mix together first 6 ingredients. Beat egg yolk; mix into mushroom mixture. Beat egg white until fluffy but not dry; fold into mushroom mixture.

Separate into six servings and fry in buttered pan until golden (about 3 minutes each side). Serve with sour cream.

Makes 6 2-inch fritters.

Other mushroom choices: Shiitake, Morel, White Button, Chanterelle, Wine-cap Stropharia.

Mushroom-Spinach Turnovers

Preheat oven to 375°F.

Sauté onion, garlic, and mushrooms in olive oil until onion is translucent and all liquid is evaporated. Stir in remaining ingredients except for packaged croissant dough. Mix to blend thoroughly.

Unroll croissant dough on floured surface. Using a rolling pin, roll into a 12- × 16-inch rectangle. Cut into 12 4-inch squares. Place a spoonful of mushroom-spinach mixture in the center of each square. Fold corners into center, overlapping and pinching to seal. Place turnovers on an ungreased baking sheet. Bake for 10–20 minutes or until golden brown. Serve immediately.

Makes 1 dozen turnovers.

Other mushroom choices: Shiitake, Morel, Wine-cap Stropharia.

½ cup finely chopped onion
1 clove garlic, minced
2 cups finely chopped Oyster mushrooms
2 tablespoons olive oil
¼ cup finely crumbled feta cheese
1 10-ounce package frozen chopped spinach, thawed
½ teaspoon black pepper
¼ teaspoon salt
¼ cup minced fresh dill
¼ cup seasoned bread crumbs
1 egg, beaten
1 package croissant roll dough

Oyster Mushroom and Sausage Bake

Butter
3 slices of bread, cubed
1 cup chopped Oyster
mushrooms
1 clove garlic, minced
2 tablespoons butter
½ pound sausage
¾ cup shredded Cheddar cheese
4 eggs
¼ cup milk

Preheat oven to 350°F.

Lightly butter the bottom of an 8- × 8-inch baking pan and cover with bread. Sauté mushrooms and garlic in butter over medium heat for approximately 5 minutes. Remove from heat.

Cook sausage and drain off fat. Combine with mushroom mixture and layer over bread. Sprinkle cheese evenly over the top. Whisk together eggs and milk, seasoning to taste with salt and pepper. Pour over contents in baking pan. Bake for 30–40 minutes or until golden brown.

Serves four. If doubled to serve eight, use a 9- × 13-inch baking pan.

Other mushroom choices: White Button, Wine-cap Stropharia, King Bolete, Morel, Shiitake.

Stuffed Tomatoes

Using a paring knife, remove tops and seeds from tomatoes creating small "bowls." Chop seeds and tops; sauté seeds and tops in olive oil along with mushrooms, onion, and garlic until all liquid has evaporated. While vegetables and mushrooms are sautéing, bring water to a boil, stir in couscous, cover, and let stand 5 minutes. If using acini di pepe, use 2 cups water, bring to a boil, and boil 8–10 minutes. Drain.

Combine mushroom mixture, undrained couscous, mint, lemon juice, and salt and pepper to taste. Stuff hollowed-out tomatoes with this mixture. Serve warm or chilled.

Serves 4.

Other mushroom choices: White Button, Wine-cap Stropharia, Shiitake.

4 medium tomatoes
2 tablespoons olive oil
1 cup finely diced Oyster mushrooms
½ cup minced onion
2 cloves garlic, minced
½ cup water
¼ cup couscous or acini di pepe
1 teaspoon dried mint flakes
1 teaspoon lemon juice

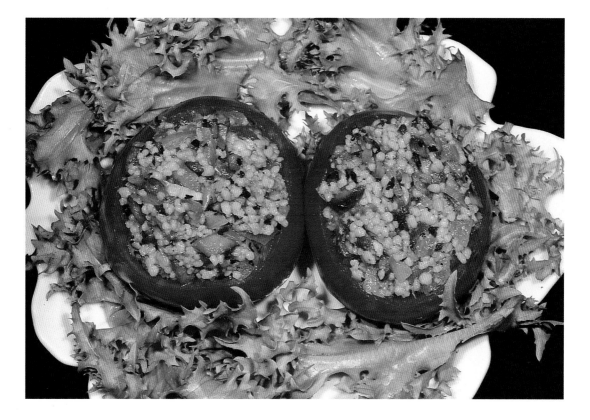

Chanterelle

Cantharellus cibarius

OTHER NAMES: Golden Chanterelle, Pfifferling.

DESCRIPTION: The cap is 1–5 inches wide, umbrella shaped and incurved when young and becoming flat with age. Often depressed at the center, it has a wavy edge. It is golden yellow to yellowish orange, smooth, moist, and firm. The stem is 1–4 inches long, tapers toward the base, and is pale yellow to yellowish orange. Yellow to yellowish orange blunt ridges are found on the undersurface of the cap. The ridges are often joined by crossveins and partially descend the stalk. The cap and stem flesh is thick, firm, yellow, and has a fruity odor. It grows on the ground in conifer or hardwood forests.

HOW SOLD: Fresh, canned, and dried.

MARKET AVAILABILITY: Fresh. Seasonally, they are available usually June to November on the East Coast and September to February on the West Coast. Dried and canned chanterelles are available year-round.

CULINARY ASPECTS: Wild.

Due to its vibrant color, apricotlike fragrance, and fruity flavor, the Chanterelle is one of the most popular of wild edible mushrooms. Its texture is delicately chewy and crunchy and holds up well in cooking. Like fruit, it is excellent with poultry of all kinds, with cheese and cream sauces, in soups and casseroles, and with eggs. To enhance its flavor, which can have peppery undertones, try combining Chanterelles with nutmeats, dried apricots, apples, or peaches. Due to the Chanterelle's sturdiness, it is excellent in baked dishes. Additionally, its color provides a nice decorative touch to meals. Although some folks enjoy eating them raw, we do not recommend it.

Use a brush and running water to clean Chanterelles. Avoid soaking them in water, or you will lose much of their flavor. Cut away debris and dried portions with a sharp knife, and check for the pres-

Opposite:
Fresh Chanterelles. Courtesy of Gourmet Mushrooms, Inc. and dried (*above*).

ence of worm holes and/or larvae. Uncleaned, Chanterelles will keep well in the refrigerator for up to a week. Cleaned they will last for a few days.

You can preserve Chanterelles by sautéing and freezing, by canning, and by drying.

COMMENTS: The popularity of the Chanterelle may be attributed to its remarkable flavor and color, its abundance in the wild, and the ease with which it can be identified. It is common throughout North America, Europe, Japan, and China. According to historical accounts, it was popular in England as far back as the eighteenth century. A use unique to the Chanterelle is the making of Chanterelle schnapps, or liquor. Soak approximately one ounce of dried Chanterelles in a fifth (750 milliliters) of vodka in a covered glass container at room temperature for 7–10 days. The mushrooms will impart their delightfully fruity flavor to the liquor, creating a fine aperitif.

Chanterelles contain considerable amounts of vitamins A and D. They have been used in Chinese medicine for the treatment of vision problems, dry skin, and respiratory infections.

Two related species are *Craterellus fallax* (Black Chanterelle) and *Craterellus cornucopioides* (Horn of Plenty). They are funnel-shaped mushrooms with a grayish brown to dark brown or nearly black upper surface. The undersurface is smooth or wrinkled and is gray or brown, sometimes with an orange tint. They are often compared to a black flower blossom, which they closely resemble. They are fine edible mushrooms with a pungent flavor and crisp texture. They are delicious fresh or dried and go particularly well with fish.

Chanterelle Popovers

Simmer Chanterelles in milk for 30 minutes. Drain and allow milk to cool. If needed, add more milk to make one cup. (Save reconstituted mushrooms to use in soups or other recipes.)

Preheat oven to 450°F.

Grease muffin tins lightly with shortening and dust with cheese. Combine milk, flour, and salt, and beat until smooth. Mix in eggs one at a time. Do not overbeat!

Fill muffin tins three-quarters full and bake for 15 minutes. Reduce heat to 350°F and bake another 20 minutes. Do not open oven before or popovers will collapse. Popovers are done when their sides are firm to the touch. Remove from oven, and pierce tops with a knife to allow steam to escape. Serve at once with butter.

Makes about 9 popovers.

Other mushroom choices: dried Morels, dried King Boletes.

1 ounce dried Chanterelles
1½ cups milk
Shortening
1 tablespoon Parmesan cheese
1 cup flour
¼ teaspoon salt
2 eggs

Mushroom and Cheese Grits

1 cup finely chopped
   Chanterelles
1 tablespoon butter
¾ cup Quaker Quick Grits
3 cups water (for thinner grits
   add more)
¼ cup grated Cheddar cheese

In a 4-cup bowl, combine mushrooms and butter and cook on High in microwave for 2½ minutes, mixing once after 1 minute. Add grits and water. Cook on High for approximately 5 minutes, until thickened. Stir in cheese.

Serves 4.

Other mushroom choices: White Button, Morel, Shiitake.

Roast Duckling with Mushroom Dressing and Apple Cider Gravy

Cut fat pads from duckling's cavity. Remove neck and giblets. Set aside. Combine next 11 ingredients and mix well. Stuff duckling with this mixture. Sew or skewer cavity openings shut. Prick skin of duckling all over. Place on rack in large pot over 1 inch of water. Cover and steam over medium heat for 1 hour.

Preheat oven to 400°F.

In a saucepan, combine water, soy sauce, marmalade, and honey. Bring to a boil; mix well and remove from heat. Baste duckling with this mixture; place duckling on a rack in a roasting pan. Bake for 20 minutes. Reduce heat to 350°F.

Baste again with soy sauce mixture. Bake an additional 15–30 minutes to desired degree of doneness. Duckling will be dark brown.

To make apple cider gravy, combine in a small saucepan cider, half and half, and 1–2 teaspoons of pan drippings. Bring to a boil, reduce heat, and simmer 15 minutes. Season to taste with salt and pepper.

Serves 4.

Other mushroom choices: Wine-cap Stropharia, King Bolete, Morel, Shiitake.

1 4½- to 5-pound duckling, thawed
2 cups finely chopped Chanterelles
½ cup finely chopped pecans
1 apple, peeled, cored, and finely chopped
¾ cup chopped onion
1 cup cooked brown rice
1 teaspoon salt
½ teaspoon pepper
1 teaspoon cinnamon
2 teaspoons minced fresh savory
½ teaspoon dried orange peel
Juice of ½ lemon
¼ cup water
2 tablespoons soy sauce
1 tablespoon orange marmalade
2 teaspoons honey
1 cup cider
¾ cup half and half

Savory Chanterelle Chowder

2 tablespoons butter
1 cup chopped onion
1 stalk celery, chopped
1 large carrot, chopped
1 cup chopped Chanterelles
2 medium potatoes, peeled and
  chopped
1 tablespoon fresh savory
  (½ teaspoon dried)
1 teaspoon chicken bouillon
  granules (or 1 cube)
1½ cups water
¼–½ cup heavy cream

Melt butter in a 3-quart saucepan. Add onion, celery, and carrot. Sauté over medium heat until onion is translucent. Add Chanterelles and continue cooking another 5 minutes. (You may substitute dried Chanterelles that have been reconstituted in milk or cream. Add milk or cream used for reconstitution at the end of the recipe, as directed.) Add potatoes, savory, bouillon, and water. Bring to a boil, reduce heat, and simmer until potatoes are tender. Season with salt and pepper to taste. Add cream and heat through without boiling.

Makes 4 1-cup servings.

Other mushroom choices: Morel, King Bolete, Shiitake, Paddy Straw, White Button.

Stuffed Pork Chops with Orange-Pineapple Glaze

8 ounces Chanterelles, finely
  chopped
¼ cup minced celery
½ cup minced onion
2 tablespoons butter
¼ cup minced fresh parsley
½ teaspoon thyme
1½ cups seasoned bread crumbs
1 egg, lightly beaten
¼–½ cup water
4 loin cut pork chops, 1½
  inches thick (about ½ pound
  each)
2 tablespoons vegetable oil
1 teaspoon beef bouillon
  granules
½ cup water
1 cup orange juice
1 teaspoon dried orange peel
1 tablespoon pineapple
  preserves
⅛ teaspoon ground cloves
1 tablespoon cornstarch,
  dissolved in 2 tablespoons
  cold water

Preheat oven to 325° F.

Sauté mushrooms, celery, and onion in butter until onion is translucent. Combine with next five ingredients, adding enough water to form a moist stuffing. Season with salt and pepper to taste.

Using a sharp knife, make a pocket in each pork chop by cutting horizontally through it almost to the bone. Fill with mushroom stuffing mixture. In a skillet, brown stuffed pork chops on each side in oil.

Place bouillon granules and ½ cup water in a baking dish. Add stuffed chops. Bake covered for 1½ hours until fork tender.

While chops are baking, combine orange juice, orange peel, pineapple preserves, and cloves in a small saucepan. Bring to a boil. Stir in cornstarch and water mixture; simmer until thickened and clear. Baste chops with glaze prior to serving.

Serves 4.

Other mushroom choices: White Button, Shiitake, Wine-cap Stropharia, White Matsutake.

Morel

Morchella esculenta

OTHER NAMES: Land Fish, Sponge Mushroom, Honeycomb Morel, Common Morel, Yellow Morel.

DESCRIPTION: The oval to elliptical, spongelike cap measures 1½–2 inches tall, ½–1½ inches wide, and has numerous irregular pits and ridges. It is pale yellow to yellowish brown and is hollow within. The brittle stem is 1–3 inches long and is also hollow. It is white with granular white ribs and is fused to the cap's edge. The cap and stem flesh is thin and white to pale yellow. It grows singly or in groups on the ground near hardwoods, in burned areas or old apple orchards, and near dead elm trees. The Black Morel (*Morchella elata*) is nearly identical but has dark brown to nearly black ridges on its cap. The White Morel (*Morchella deliciosa*) is also nearly identical but has white ridges and grayish pits.

HOW SOLD: Fresh and dried.

MARKET AVAILABILITY: Fresh Morels are available seasonally, usually March through May. Dried ones are available year-round.

CULINARY ASPECTS: Wild.

The Morel is one of the most popular and sought-after of wild mushrooms. It is also one of the earliest mushrooms to appear in the spring, often fruiting while snow is still present. Its flavor and texture are unlike those of any other mushroom, tasting nutlike or meaty with a texture both crisp and chewy. It has an aromatic quality that lends itself nicely to light cream or wine sauces, egg dishes, and pasta. Because of its unique and robust flavor, take care to use mild-flavored recipes that allow the Morel to stand out and be complemented, rather than overwhelmed. The whole mushroom, cap and stem, is edible. Since it is hollow, it makes a fine vehicle for stuffings. Its texture is firm enough to make baking an excellent cooking method. An important word of caution: the Morel should *never* be eaten raw!

Opposite:
Dried Morels and fresh (*above*).

Eating Morels raw can cause particularly acute gastrointestinal illness, including painful indigestion, nausea, vomiting, and diarrhea.

To clean fresh Morels, avoid using water, which reduces flavor. A brush works well in cleaning debris, usually sand or grit, from their pits and ridges. If you must use water, rinse them under it quickly, and dry them on paper toweling. If you are stuffing whole Morels, check the interior cavity for insects and debris; otherwise, cut Morels lengthwise, and check the interior for unwanted critters.

Morels dry very well, so drying is an excellent way to preserve them. To reconstitute dried Morels, soak them in warm water for 20–30 minutes. As an alternative, try reconstituting them in milk or cream by simmering them in it, without bringing the mixture to a boil, for the same amount of time. Use the liquid as well as the mushrooms in your cooking. The extract derived from reconstituting Morels in water can be stored for future use by freezing. Some folks recommend sautéing and freezing Morels, but we much prefer drying them for later use.

COMMENTS: The popularity of the Morel is a cause for celebration in areas where it is abundant. Both Michigan and Minnesota hold festivals to welcome its arrival. People have even burned areas of forests in attempts to duplicate its favored habitat of burn sites. This became so much of a problem in parts of Europe that governments passed special laws forbidding such practices.

There is a story told about a witch who, when arguing with the Devil, so angered him that he grabbed her, chopped her up into multiple pieces, and threw her to the wind. Wherever a piece of her landed, a little wrinkled mushroom appeared that looked like her wrinkled face—the Morel! That witch must have been a good witch, considering the deliciousness of her "offspring"!

Grilled Trout Stuffed with Morels and Spring Greens

Melt butter in saucepan; add Morels, watercress, garlic, dill, and scallions. Mix, cover, and cook over low heat for 5–10 minutes. Mix in remaining ingredients except trout.

Stuff trout with vegetable mixture. Brush sides with vegetable oil or melted butter. Grill for approximately 5–7 minutes each side. Alternate cooking method: Bake at 350°F for approximately 10 minutes each side, turning once.

Serves 2.

Other mushroom choices: White Button, Wine-cap Stropharia, Shiitake, Oyster, Enokitake.

1 tablespoon butter
1 cup finely chopped Morels
1 bunch watercress, finely
   chopped (about 2 cups)
1 clove garlic, minced
1 tablespoon minced fresh dill
4 scallions with tops, minced
½–1 teaspoon prepared
   horseradish
½ teaspoon salt
¼ teaspoon freshly ground
   black pepper
2 tablespoons cracker meal
2 8-ounce trout (serving size)
Vegetable oil or melted butter

Morel and Smoked Oyster Sauce

4 ounces fresh Morels, sliced
(about 1½ cups)
4 tablespoons butter
1 teaspoon chicken bouillon
granules (one cube)
1½ cups water
4 tablespoons flour
1 cup light cream
2 ounces Fontina cheese,
shredded
1 3¾–ounce can smoked whole
oysters

Sauté Morels in 1 tablespoon butter over medium heat for 5–8 minutes. Dissolve chicken bouillon in water and set aside. Melt 3 tablespoons butter in a 2-quart saucepan. Stir in flour and cook over medium-high heat, stirring constantly, for 2–3 minutes. Whisk in water and chicken bouillon. Add cream and simmer, stirring constantly, over low heat until thickened and smooth. Do not allow to boil! Stir in cheese, Morels, and oysters. Season to taste with salt and pepper. Serve over pasta, cooked grains, vegetables, or fish.

Makes approximately 3 cups of sauce.

Other mushroom choices: Chanterelle, White Button, Shiitake, Winecap Stropharia.

Morel Sauce

Place Morels, soy sauce, and water in a saucepan; bring to a boil; reduce heat and simmer 30–45 minutes. Remove Morels, reserving liquid. Chop Morels finely.

Sauté shallots, savory, and Morels in butter for 2–3 minutes. Stir in flour and then liquid from reconstituting Morels. Simmer until thickened, mixing often. Add salt and pepper to taste, and then add sour cream. Heat without boiling.

Serve over beef, pork, veal, vegetables, or hot buttered noodles.

Makes about 2 cups.

Other mushroom choices: dried King Boletes, dried Chanterelles.

1 ounce dried Morels
2 teaspoons soy sauce
2 cups water
4 tablespoons finely chopped
  shallots
2 teaspoons minced fresh savory
3 tablespoons butter
1½ tablespoons flour
¾ cup sour cream

Mushroom and Ham Cheesecake

7⅓ tablespoons butter
1⅓ cups cracker crumbs
8 ounces Morels, sliced ¼-inch thick
2 8-ounce packages cream cheese, softened
3 eggs
¼ cup flour
8 ounces sour cream
2 teaspoons curry powder
¼ teaspoon salt
2 tablespoons grated onion
6 ounces Swiss cheese, shredded
½ cup diced Cappicola ham (about 2–3 ounces)

Preheat oven to 300°F.

Melt ⅓ cup (5⅓ tablespoons) butter and combine with cracker crumbs. Press on bottom and 1 inch up the sides of a 9-inch springform pan. Set aside.

Sauté sliced mushrooms in remaining 2 tablespoons butter until all liquid has evaporated. Set aside.

Beat cream cheese at high speed until light and fluffy. Beat in eggs, one at a time. Add flour and sour cream, beating well. Beat in curry powder and salt. By hand, mix in onion and Swiss cheese.

Pour one-third of mixture into prepared springform pan. Sprinkle ham evenly over top. Pour in half of remaining mixture. Layer mushrooms evenly over top. Top with remaining cream cheese mixture.

Bake 45–60 minutes, until set. Turn heat off, partially open door, and allow cheesecake to cool in oven for 1 hour. Serve immediately, or cool and chill completely. May be eaten chilled or warm.

Serves 8–10.

Other mushroom choices: White Button, Wine-cap Stropharia, Shiitake, Chanterelle.

Photo shows alternate mushroom choice.

Pesto and Mushroom Lasagna

Preheat oven to 350°F.

In a saucepan, melt 2 tablespoons butter, whisk in flour; cook 3 minutes over medium heat. Whisk in milk and bouillon, add red pepper flakes, and cook until slightly thickened. Set aside.

Sauté mushrooms in 2 tablespoons butter until they begin to release their juices (about 5 minutes); stir in dried basil, salt, and pepper. In a bowl, mix together egg, ricotta cheese, and pesto.

Using a 9- × 9-inch baking pan, place a small amount of sauce in bottom of pan. Layer noodles (cutting to fit pan), ricotta cheese mixture, grated mozzarella cheese, and sautéed mushrooms. Repeat, in that order, making three layers. Place remaining noodle pieces on top. Pour remaining sauce over the top, and sprinkle with Parmesan cheese.

Bake for about 35–40 minutes until it is bubbly and just beginning to brown on the edges.

Serves 6–9.

Other mushroom choices: White Button, Shiitake, Wine-cap Stropharia, White Matsutake.

4 tablespoons butter
2 tablespoons flour
1½ cups milk
½ cup vegetable bouillon or stock
¼ teaspoon crushed red pepper flakes
8–10 ounces Morels, sliced ¼-inch thick
1 teaspoon dried basil
½ teaspoon salt
¼ teaspoon black pepper
1 egg, lightly beaten
1 pound ricotta cheese
4 ounces basil pesto
9 lasagna noodles, cooked until barely tender (about 5 minutes)
8 ounces mozzarella cheese, grated
Parmesan cheese

Photo shows alternate mushroom choice.

JW

Paddy Straw Mushroom

Volvariella volvacea

JW

OTHER NAMES: Chinese Mushroom, Straw Mushroom, Padi-Straw Mushroom.

DESCRIPTION: The cultivated variety of the Paddy Straw mushroom is commercially available as unexpanded buttons covered by a veil of tissue (unpeeled mushrooms) or as expanded buttons (peeled mushrooms). When unexpanded, they are oval, egg-shaped mushrooms. They are whitish to pale tan and measure 1–1½ inches long. Expanded buttons have a cone-shaped to umbrella-shaped cap measuring ¾–1¼ inches wide. Caps are tan with a brownish black center and blackish streaks. Stems are short, ½–1¼ inches long, tan, and enlarged at the base. They are attached to the center of the cap. Pale yellow gills are found on the undersurface of the cap. The cap and stem flesh is also pale yellow. This mushroom is cultivated on rice straw.

HOW SOLD: Canned and dried.

MARKET AVAILABILITY: Year-round.

CULINARY ASPECTS: Cultivated and wild.

In Chinese restaurants, this is the little mushroom most frequently found hiding among the vegetables, meats, and fish. For that reason,

Opposite:
Paddy Straw mushrooms as they come from the can and as seen in nature in the button and in the more mature form (*above* and *above left*).

it is one of the more commonly encountered mushrooms, even though its name often remains unknown. Mildly flavored and versatile, the Paddy Straw mushroom can be used with nearly any type of food. It has a smooth and delicate texture and has a pleasing appearance. The entire mushroom is edible. The unpeeled stage is more strongly flavored than the expanded, or peeled, stage. When cooked, it retains a pocket of heated juices within its membranous veil that is a delicious, though potentially burning, treat. Dried Paddy Straw mushrooms, like many other mushrooms, are more intensely flavored than fresh or canned forms. Regardless of the type used, little cooking is required. Merely heat them through by adding them to recipes during the final stages of cooking. They can be successfully pickled or used in casseroles, stir-fry recipes, or marinades.

Before using canned Paddy Straw mushrooms, discard the fluid they were stored in and rinse them thoroughly. Dried mushrooms should be inspected for evidence of insects or larvae and then rinsed with water. Unused canned mushrooms can be stored covered by water in a closed container in the refrigerator for 7–10 days. Change water every 2–3 days.

COMMENTS: The Paddy Straw mushroom earned its name because it occurs naturally on decomposing rice straw stacks in Southeast Asia. Its use and cultivation in China date back approximately two thousand years. Attempts to grow it on a commercial scale in the United States have not been successful. Of the commercially available mushrooms, the Paddy Straw mushroom ranks third in consumption worldwide. Because of its vitamin C, protein, and amino acid content, using it to supplement diets that are otherwise low in protein seems reasonable. It has been used in Chinese medicine to prevent scurvy and infectious diseases and to heal wounds.

Creamed Paddy Straw Mushrooms with Baby Peas

Sauté onion in butter until translucent. Stir in frozen peas and drained mushrooms. Cook over medium-high heat for approximately 3–5 minutes, stirring frequently. Dice prosciutto and add along with the bouillon, cream, salt, and cornstarch dissolved in water to the peas and mushrooms. Simmer, mixing often, until thickened (about 3 minutes). Add pepper to taste.

Serves 4–6.

Other mushroom choices: Sliced and sautéed White Buttons, Morels, King Boletes, Wine-cap Stropharias, Chanterelles.

2 tablespoons minced onion
1 tablespoon butter
1 9-ounce package frozen baby peas
1 15-ounce can Paddy Straw mushrooms, drained and rinsed
1 ounce prosciutto
1 teaspoon chicken bouillon (or one cube)
¼ cup cream or milk
¼ teaspoon salt
1 tablespoon cornstarch, dissolved in ½ cup water

Dragon's Mist Soup

1 13- to 15-ounce can chicken
  broth
1½ cups water
4 cloves garlic, finely minced
2 scallions with tops, minced
½ cup bamboo shoots, drained
  and rinsed, cut into
  matchstick-size pieces
1 15-ounce can Paddy Straw
  mushrooms, drained and
  rinsed
2 tablespoons soy sauce
1 teaspoon salt
¼ teaspoon white pepper
5 ounces tofu, cut into ½-inch
  cubes
1 teaspoon sesame oil

In a saucepan, combine broth, water, and garlic. Bring to a boil, reduce heat, and simmer 10 minutes. Add all remaining ingredients except sesame oil. Return to boil, reduce heat, and simmer 5 minutes. Just before serving, stir in sesame oil.

Serves 4.

Other mushroom choices: 2 cups sliced fresh White Button, Shiitake, Wine-cap Stropharia, Enokitake, or Oyster, or 1 cup sliced fresh White Matsutake. Sauté fresh mushrooms lightly in vegetable oil prior to adding to soup. May also use 1 cup reconstituted Wood Ears, cut into 1-inch pieces, without sautéing.

Garlic Shrimp with Mushrooms

In a medium-sized bowl, combine first eight ingredients. Add shrimp and mix to coat well. Allow to marinate at room temperature for 15 minutes, mixing occasionally. Heat wok or large nonstick skillet over medium-high heat. Add vegetable oil, shrimp mixture, and snow pea pods to wok; stir-fry over high heat until shrimp turn pink and pea pods are bright green. Add mushrooms and heat through. Serve over noodles or cooked rice. Garnish with minced green onion tops.

Makes 4 servings.

Other mushroom choices: Fresh Enokitake; sautéed Shiitake, White Button or White Matsutake.

3 green onions, minced (save tops for garnish)
3 tablespoons soy sauce
2 tablespoons wine vinegar
4 large cloves garlic, minced
2 teaspoons minced fresh ginger
4 teaspoons sesame oil
2 teaspoons sugar
½ teaspoon crushed red pepper flakes
1 pound shrimp, peeled and deveined
2 tablespoons vegetable oil
1 cup fresh snow pea pods
1 15-ounce can Paddy Straw mushrooms, drained and rinsed
Somen or lo mein noodles (egg noodles or cooked rice may be substituted)

Photo shows alternate mushroom choice.

Marinated Mushrooms and Fiddlehead Ferns

1¼ pounds (about 6 cups) fiddleheads
1 15-ounce can Paddy Straw mushrooms
½ cup chopped onion
2 cloves garlic, minced
½ cup red wine vinegar
1 tablespoon sugar
1 teaspoon dried tarragon
2 teaspoons Dijon-style mustard
¼ cup white wine
¾ cup vegetable oil
¼ cup chopped roasted sweet red peppers

Clean fiddleheads and steam as you would asparagus until tender (about 20 minutes); drain and set aside. Drain mushrooms, rinse under cold water, and set aside.

Place onion, garlic, vinegar, sugar, and tarragon in a small saucepan. Bring to a boil. Reduce heat and simmer covered 10 minutes. Remove from heat. Add mustard, wine, and oil; mix until well blended.

Combine fiddleheads, mushrooms, and roasted red peppers in a non-corrosive container. Cover with marinade, mix well, and add salt and pepper to taste. Cover container and allow to cool to room temperature before refrigerating. Serve chilled.

Makes about 2 quarts.

Marinated Mushrooms and Herring

In a saucepan combine all ingredients except mushrooms, herring, and sour cream. Bring to a boil. Add mushrooms; reduce heat; and simmer 5 minutes, mixing once or twice while cooking. Place in covered bowl and refrigerate several hours or overnight.

Serve with pickled herring and sour cream.

Makes approximately 3 cups.

Other mushroom choice: canned White Button mushroom caps.

⅓ cup red wine vinegar
⅓ cup vegetable oil
1 cup coarsely chopped onion
1 teaspoon salt
¼ cup minced parsley
1 tablespoon minced dill weed
1 teaspoon dry mustard
2 tablespoons maple syrup
1 15-ounce can Paddy Straw mushrooms, drained and rinsed
1 8-ounce jar pickled herring
Sour cream (optional)

Photo shows alternate mushroom choice.

OTHER NAMES: Tree Ear, Black Fungus, Judas' Ear.

DESCRIPTION: When fresh or reconstituted, this mushroom resembles a large ear or an irregular cup. It is wrinkled, shiny, and measures 1–6 inches in diameter. The upper surface is purplish gray, becoming nearly black with age. The lower surface is pale pinkish gray and covered with fine hair. It darkens toward the base. The flesh is thin, gelatinous, and dark purplish gray to black. When dried, this mushroom becomes shriveled and irregularly folded. It is hard and is dark brown to black on the upper surface and grayish brown below. The Cloud Ear (*Auricularia auricula*) is very similar, but is somewhat smaller: 1–4½ inches wide, thinner, pinkish brown to dark reddish brown, and lacks fine hair. Both species grow singly or in clusters on wood.

HOW SOLD: Dried and fresh.

MARKET AVAILABILITY: Year-round.

CULINARY ASPECTS: Cultivated and wild.

This mushroom is famous for its texture and color, rather than for its flavor, which is so mild as to be faint. The flesh is gelatinous, firm, and crunchy even after being rehydrated and cooked. It is an excellent choice for stir-fry dishes, soups, and salads when a touch of contrast is desired. It requires minimal cooking. It is best when added during the final moment of cooking or mixed into foods that are prepared and hot and allowed to stand for a few minutes. It lends itself well to onion, garlic, leeks, and scallions.

To reconstitute dried Wood Ear mushrooms, bring them to a boil in water, remove them from heat, allow them to stand for 30–60 minutes, drain, and discard the water. Trim fibrous and tough portions away, and rinse the mushrooms under running water. Once rehydrated, the Wood Ear can expand up to five times its dried size. Take this into consideration when planning serving sizes.

Fresh Wood Ear and Cloud Ear mushrooms are best preserved by drying.

COMMENTS: The Wood Ear and Cloud Ear are being studied for their effects on blood. They contain a chemical compound that inhibits blood clotting. This mushroom may prove beneficial in preventing such diseases as stroke and heart attacks. The Chinese believe that consuming this mushroom, brewed in a tea or eaten regularly as part of the diet, enhances health and cures such ailments as headaches.

Wood Ear

Auricularia polytricha

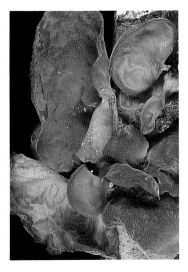

Opposite:
Dried Wood Ears and fresh (*above*).

Mixed Mushroom Sauce

1 cup boiling water
¼ cup dried Wood Ear mushrooms
⅓ cup dried Chanterelles, Morels, or King Boletes
1 large clove garlic, minced
2 tablespoons minced shallot
1 tablespoon butter
1 teaspoon vegetable bouillon granules, dissolved in 1 cup boiling water
½ cup white wine
2 cups cream, or half and half
¼ cup grated Edam cheese
1 tablespoon flour, dissolved in 2 tablespoons water

In a small bowl, pour boiling water over mushrooms; set aside for 20–30 minutes. Sauté garlic and shallot in butter until translucent. Add vegetable bouillon and wine, bring to a boil, and then reduce heat and simmer 15 minutes. Drain mushrooms, reserving liquid. Chop mushrooms coarsely. Add mushrooms and their liquid to sauce, along with the cream. Return to a boil. Reduce heat and boil gently for 30 minutes, mixing occasionally. Stir in cheese, and salt and pepper to taste. Whisk in flour and water mixture, cooking over medium-low heat until thickened.

Serve hot over chicken, fish, or vegetables.

Makes about 2 cups.

Oriental Chicken and Pasta

Cover Wood Ear mushrooms with hot water, cover with lid, and allow to stand 20–30 minutes. Drain and chop coarsely. Set aside.

Sauté onions, green pepper, celery, garlic, and chicken in oil over medium-high heat, stirring often, for 3–5 minutes. Add bouillon, ginger, and pasta. Bring to a boil, reduce to simmer, and then cover and cook until pasta is tender (about 12–15 minutes). Stir in drained mushrooms, water chestnuts, and soy sauce. Heat through.

Serves 4–6.

Other mushroom choices: Paddy Straw, sautéed White Matsutake, grated or shaved Black Truffle.

½ ounce dried Wood Ear mushrooms
5 green onions with tops, coarsely chopped
½ cup coarsely chopped green pepper
1 stalk celery, coarsely chopped
1 large clove garlic, minced
2 cups (about ½ pound) chicken, cut into ½-inch strips
2 tablespoons vegetable oil
2 teaspoons chicken bouillon granules, dissolved in 2½ cups water
2 teaspoons grated fresh ginger
8 ounces (1¼ cups) acini di pepe pasta
½ cup sliced water chestnuts
2 teaspoons soy sauce

Thai Soup with Wood Ears

1 tablespoon dried Wood Ear
  mushrooms
1 cup boiling water
1 large clove garlic, minced
1 teaspoon grated fresh ginger
1 tablespoon vegetable oil
1 8-ounce bottle clam juice
1 1.8-ounce package Knorr
  Leek Soup Mix
1 cup water
1 14-ounce can coconut milk
1 dried chili pepper with seeds,
  crushed
¼ teaspoon tumeric
Juice of 1 lime
2 tablespoons minced cilantro
  for garnish

Stir Wood Ear mushrooms into boiling water. Set aside for 20–30 minutes.

Sauté garlic and ginger briefly in oil, being careful not to burn them. Whisk in clam juice, soup mix, and 1 cup water. Bring to a boil. Reduce heat and simmer 10 minutes.

Drain mushrooms and chop coarsely. Add to soup, along with coconut milk and tumeric. Add chili pepper gradually to taste. Simmer 10 minutes. Stir in lime juice. Serve hot, garnished with minced cilantro.

Serves 4 as an appetizer.

Other mushroom choices: Paddy Straw, sautéed White Matsutake.

Tropical Fruit Salad

Cut mushrooms into thin strips, about 1 inch long and ¼ inch wide. In a large bowl, combine all ingredients and mix well. Serve chilled or at room temperature.

Serves 4.

Other mushroom choice: fresh Enokitake.

¼ cup reconstituted (about ¼ ounce dried) Wood Ear mushrooms
1 papaya, peeled, seeded, and cut into 1-inch pieces
1 large avocado, peeled, pitted, and cut into 1-inch pieces
3 scallions with tops, chopped
1 tablespoon minced fresh cilantro
1 tablespoon Rose's Lime Juice
1 teaspoon jalapeño sauce
1 tablespoon balsamic vinegar

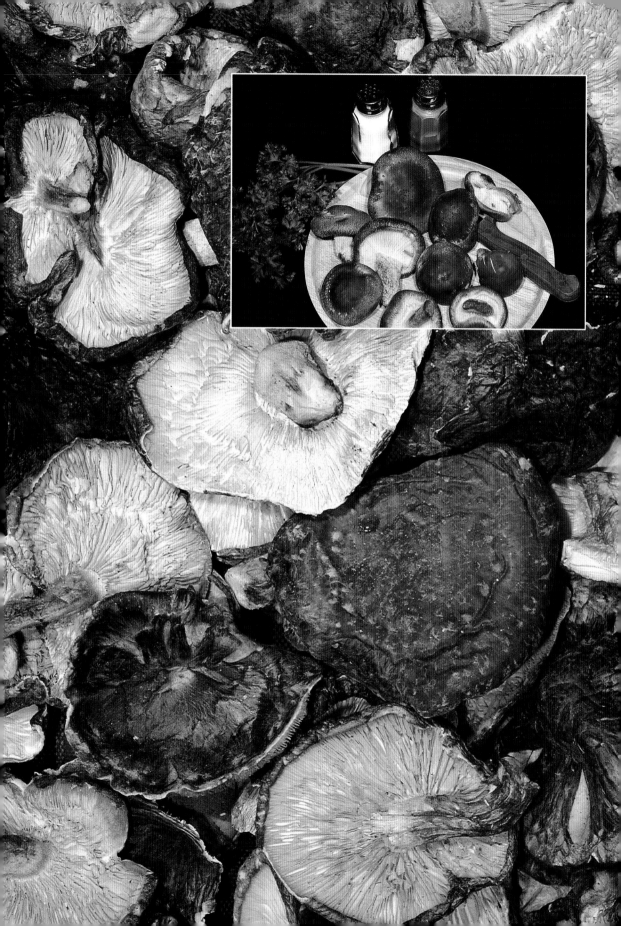

Shiitake

Lentinula edodes

OTHER NAMES: *Lentinus edodes,* Japanese Black Mushroom, Chinese Black Mushroom, Black Forest Mushroom (trade name), Doubloon (trade name), Golden Oak Mushroom.

DESCRIPTION: The cap is 2–6 inches wide, umbrella shaped with an inrolled edge when young but nearly flat with age. It is pale pinkish brown to dark reddish brown and dry. The edge is covered with tiny, flattened, whitish, cottony patches. The tough and fibrous stem is 1–3 inches long and is typically attached to the center of the cap. It is white to pale pinkish brown and is often coated with tiny white hair. Creamy white gills are found on the undersurface of the cap. The cap and stem flesh is firm and white. It grows in clusters on hardwoods, especially oak, beech, and chestnut.

HOW SOLD: Fresh, dried.

MARKET AVAILABILITY: Year-round.

CULINARY ASPECTS: Cultivated and wild.

This is an all-purpose mushroom that is excellent with all foods. It can be used in soups, sauces, casseroles, and duxelles and for braising and frying. Its flesh is hardy enough to withstand long cooking, and its flavor and aroma are strong enough to be complemented by intense spices such as garlic, coriander, and various peppers. Its flavor is often considered rich and smoky. While the flesh of the cap is meaty, the stems are often tough and inedible. When shopping for Shiitake, choose mushrooms that have caps 2–3 inches in diameter and relatively small stems. Use the stems for making broths, soup stocks, sauces, and gravies. Fresh Shiitake require minimal cleaning because they grow on wood or wood-product substrates. Simply brush or wipe clean with a mushroom brush or cloth. Cut stems away from caps.

To reconstitute dried Shiitake, cover them with water and add 1 tablespoon soy sauce. Bring to a boil, cover, and remove from heat. Let stand for 20–30 minutes or overnight in the refrigerator. Use liquid in recipes along with mushroom caps.

Fresh Shiitake mushrooms are best preserved by drying. They may also be sautéed and then frozen.

COMMENTS: The Shiitake grows wild over all of eastern Asia. Documents refer to its cultivation and use in China as long as two thousand years ago. It is presently the second most commonly cultivated mushroom in the world. Shiitake contain lentinan, a complex sugar. Recent research indicates that lentinan has anticancer properties. Shiitake also contain two other compounds that have been shown to have anticholesterol and antiviral properties.

Opposite:
Dried Shiitake mushrooms and fresh (*insert*).

Mushroom Salsa

2 tablespoons butter
1 cup minced onion
2 cloves garlic, minced
2 teaspoons finely minced fresh
   jalapeño
1½ cups finely chopped Shiitake
1 cup chopped fresh tomatoes
¼ teaspoon salt
1 teaspoon red wine vinegar
½ teaspoon sugar

In a saucepan, melt butter and add onion, garlic, and jalapeño. Sauté until onion is translucent, being careful not to brown garlic. Add mushrooms and cook over medium heat, mixing occasionally, for 5 minutes. Add tomatoes and continue cooking over medium heat an additional 5 minutes. Add salt, vinegar, and sugar. Simmer 5 minutes.

Serve hot with eggs, meat, or fish.

Makes about 2 cups.

Other mushroom choices: White Button, Wine-cap Stropharia, King Bolete.

Photo shows alternate mushroom choice.

Aunt Ruth's Lamb and Mushroom Curry

BY RUTH RAINIS

In a large skillet or pan, sauté onions, garlic, and mushrooms in oil until onion is translucent. Add tomato paste, curry paste, and chicken broth. Mix well. Add ginger and simmer a few minutes. Add lamb. Simmer covered over low heat for about an hour, mixing occasionally to prevent sticking on the bottom. Add peas and simmer 5–7 minutes more.

Serve over rice and garnish with fried onions. Chutney makes a nice accompaniment.

Serves 6.

Other mushroom choices: White Button, Wine-cap Stropharia, White Matsutake.

2 large onions, chopped
4 large cloves garlic, minced
2 cups chopped Shiitake mushrooms
3 tablespoons oil
1 12-ounce can tomato paste
2–3 tablespoons curry paste
1 13- to 15-ounce can chicken broth
1 teaspoon fresh grated ginger
2 pounds lamb, cut into 1½-inch pieces
1 10-ounce package frozen baby green peas
Cooked rice or rice pilaf
Fried onions

Seasoned Steamed Clams and Mushrooms

4 cups Shiitake, sliced ½ inch
thick (¾ pound)
¼ cup butter or margarine
1 cup chopped onion (large
chunks)
1 cup coarsely chopped celery
1 cup sliced carrots (¼-inch
rounds)
2 large cloves garlic, minced
¼ cup minced fresh parsley
1 bay leaf
1 13- to 15-ounce can chicken
broth
½ teaspoon dried basil
¼ teaspoon white pepper
2 tablespoons dry vermouth
4 dozen hard-shell clams

Sauté mushrooms in 2 tablespoons butter over medium-high heat for 3–5 minutes, mixing constantly. Set aside.

In a 6-quart saucepan melt remaining butter. Add onion, celery, carrots, and garlic. Sauté, mixing frequently, over medium-low heat until onion is translucent. Add remaining ingredients, except for clams and mushrooms; simmer covered 5 minutes. Add clams and mushrooms and return to boil. Cover and reduce heat. Simmer approximately 10 minutes or until clams are all opened, stirring once at halfway point to ensure even cooking.

Serve with crusty garlic bread and a light white wine.

Serves 4.

Other mushroom choices: White Button, White Matsutake, Oyster.

Photo shows alternate mushroom choice.

Shiitake Frittata

BY MALCOLM CLARK

Preheat oven to 325°F.

Sauté onion, garlic, and Shiitake in olive oil, over medium heat, until barely limp; add to beaten eggs. Combine with all remaining ingredients, mixing well. Turn into buttered 7- × 11-inch pan. Bake for about 30 minutes, or until firm and lightly browned. Cool and cut into 1-inch squares.

Makes about 6 dozen 1-inch squares.

Other mushroom choices: White Button, Morel, Chanterelle.

1 medium onion, diced
1 clove garlic, minced
8 ounces fresh Shiitake
   mushrooms, finely diced
3 tablespoons olive oil
6 eggs, beaten
¼ cup bread crumbs
½ teaspoon salt
⅛ teaspoon each: oregano,
   white pepper, Tabasco
½ pound Monterey Jack cheese,
   grated
2 tablespoons finely chopped
   fresh cilantro

OTHER NAMES: Enoki, Golden Needles, Winter Mushroom, Christmas Mushroom, Velvet Foot.

DESCRIPTION: The cap of the cultivated variety is very small (¼–1 inch wide), umbrella shaped and incurved when young but flattened with age. It is pale yellow to orange-yellow, smooth, shiny, and firm. Stems are 3–5 inches long and are tough and fibrous toward the base where they are joined together. This gives them the appearance of fused matchsticks. They are very thin, pale yellow, and attached to the center of the cap. White to pale yellow gills are found on the undersurface of the cap. The cap and stem flesh is thin and white to pale yellow. Enokitakes are cultivated on enriched wheat straw.

The wild variety, commonly called the Velvet Foot, differs from the cultivated form. It has a 1- to 3-inch, bright orange-yellow to brownish-orange sticky cap. The stem is 1–3 inches long; is reddish brown; and is densely coated with short, velvety, brown to brownish black hair. It grows in clusters on hardwoods, especially on elm, willow, and aspen.

HOW SOLD: Fresh, canned, or bottled.

MARKET AVAILABILITY: Year-round.

CULINARY ASPECTS: Cultivated and wild.

This fragile little mushroom is known for its appearance, as well as its mild flavor. Often described as radishlike or peppery, it complements salads and soups both as a main ingredient and as a garnish. You may eat this mushroom raw, but be certain that the mushrooms are crisp and rigid. If they are soggy or discolored, discard them. Because of their delicate nature, they require almost no cooking: just a minute or so, no more. They are a beautiful visual addition floating on top of consommé or peeking out in stir-fry dishes.

To clean fresh Enokitake, trim away the lower, fibrous portions of the stem. Rinse quickly under water. If using canned varieties, discard liquid and rinse mushrooms under water. They will keep for up to a week refrigerated.

COMMENTS: The cultivated variety of Enokitake is imported almost exclusively from Japan. The wild variety, which is widely distributed throughout the world, fruits into late fall and winter. Even after being frozen and thawed out, the mushrooms can continue to grow normally. This is why Enokitake is called the Winter or Christmas Mushroom. An anticancer compound found in some wood-decomposing fungi has also been isolated from Enokitakes. This mushroom has been used in Chinese medicine and is claimed to prevent and cure certain liver diseases and stomach ulcers.

Enokitake

Flammulina velutipes

Opposite:
Fresh cultivated Enokitakes and the wild alternate form (*above*).

Baked Fish Fillets with Enokitake

1 10-ounce can Enokitake
  mushrooms
¼ cup flour
¼ cup plus 1 tablespoon grated
  Parmesan cheese
½ cup seasoned bread crumbs
¼ teaspoon each salt and black
  pepper
1 pound fish fillets (scrod,
  orange roughy, or haddock)
1 egg, lightly beaten with
  1 tablespoon milk
1 tablespoon lemon juice
3 tablespoons butter, melted
Paprika

Preheat oven to 350°F.

Drain and rinse mushrooms; set aside. Combine flour, ¼ cup Parmesan cheese, bread crumbs, and salt and pepper in a shallow dish. Dip fish fillets in egg wash; dredge in flour mixture; place in lightly buttered baking dish. Save remaining egg wash and set aside. Combine lemon juice and melted butter. Reserving about 1 tablespoon, sprinkle evenly over fish. Set aside remaining butter and lemon juice.

Bake fish for approximately 20 minutes, or until lightly browned. Mix mushrooms in remaining egg wash. Arrange around fish. Sprinkle with 1 tablespoon Parmesan cheese and remaining butter–lemon juice mixture. Sprinkle paprika over all. Return to oven and bake an additional 10 minutes.

Serves 4.

Other mushroom choices: Paddy Straw; sautéed Morels or Wine-cap Stropharia.

Enokitake and Endive Salad

Arrange Belgian endive and Enokitake on salad plates. Sprinkle with walnuts. Combine oil, vinegar, and salt; mix well; and sprinkle over salads. Top with freshly ground black pepper.

Serves 2.

Other mushroom choices: Reconstituted and slivered Wood Ear, thinly sliced White Button.

2 heads Belgian endive, quartered lengthwise
1 ounce fresh Enokitake, cleaned and trimmed
¼ cup coarsely chopped walnuts
½ cup vegetable oil
¼ cup raspberry vinegar
¼ teaspoon salt
Freshly ground black pepper

Mushroom- and Herb-stuffed Chicken Rolls with Cranberry Glaze

1½–2 pounds boneless and skinless chicken breasts
1 cup finely chopped Enokitake
1 stalk celery, minced
1 cup minced bok choy (Chinese cabbage or celery cabbage may be substituted)
2 green onions with tops, minced
2 tablespoons vegetable oil
1–2 teaspoons ginger, grated
1 teaspoon cooking sherry
½ cup herb-seasoned stuffing mix
½ cup water
½ cup dry white wine
3 tablespoons jellied cranberry sauce
1 tablespoon frozen orange juice concentrate

Place chicken breasts, one at a time, between layers of waxed paper and pound with a rolling pin or other utensil until ¼ inch thick and nearly translucent. Set aside.

In a large skillet, sauté mushrooms, celery, bok choy, and onions in oil over medium-high heat for 10 minutes, stirring frequently. Add ginger, sherry, and stuffing mix. Mix well and remove from heat.

Spread mushroom mixture evenly over each flattened chicken breast. Roll lengthwise like a jelly roll and secure by tying with string or un-waxed dental floss. Place in large skillet, add water and wine, and bring to a boil. Reduce heat, cover, and simmer for 20 minutes.

While chicken is cooking, make glaze by combining cranberry sauce and orange juice concentrate in a small saucepan. Mix well and bring to a boil. Reduce heat and keep warm.

Remove string from chicken. Cut into ½-inch slices. Serve with cranberry glaze.

Serves 4.

Other mushroom choices: White Button, Shiitake, Chanterelle, Winecap Stropharia, Oyster.

Stir-fry Beef with Enokitake Mushrooms

Chill steak in freezer until it is firm, and slice it into ⅛-inch strips. Combine sugar, water, soy sauce, sherry, and ginger in a bowl. Add beef, mix well, and set aside. Drain mushrooms, rinse briefly under water, and set aside.

Heat 1 tablespoon of oil in a wok or large nonstick skillet. Add pea pods, water chestnuts, garlic, and scallions. Stir-fry for 2 minutes over medium-high heat; remove to a plate and set aside. Add remaining tablespoon of oil to wok, add beef and soy sauce mixture, and stir-fry 2 minutes. Add mushrooms and previously set aside vegetables. Bring to a boil. Stir in cornstarch and water. Cook, stirring constantly, until thickened. Serve over rice or noodles (e.g., cellophane or Chinese egg noodles).

Serves 4.

Other mushroom choices: Paddy Straw, sliced White Button, sliced Matsutake, reconstituted and sliced Wood Ear.

1 pound sirloin or other steak
2 teaspoons sugar
¼ cup water
¼ cup soy sauce or tamari
2 tablespoons sherry
1 tablespoon grated ginger
1 10- to 15-ounce can Enokitake mushrooms
2 tablespoons peanut oil
1 cup fresh snow pea pods (or frozen, thawed)
¼ cup water chestnuts, drained and sliced ¼-inch thick
2 cloves garlic, minced
2 scallions with tops, chopped
1 tablespoon cornstarch, dissolved in 2 tablespoons water

White Matsutake

Tricholoma magnivelare

OTHER NAMES: *Armillaria ponderosa,* American Pine Mushroom.

DESCRIPTION: The cap is 2–8 inches wide, umbrella shaped with a cottony inrolled edge when young but nearly flat with age. It is white to creamy white and smooth at first but soon becomes pale yellowish brown with darker reddish brown flattened scales. The stem is 2–6 inches long, very thick and firm, and typically tapered toward the base. It is white, covered by patches of pale reddish brown tissue below a white cottony ring, and attached to the center of the cap. White to pale yellow gills that turn pale brown when bruised are found on the undersurface of the cap. The cap and stem flesh is thick, firm, white, and fragrant. White Matsutake grows singly or in groups on soil under conifers, especially fir and hemlock.

HOW SOLD: Fresh and dried.

MARKET AVAILABILITY: The availability of fresh White Matsutake depends on region as well as season. These mushrooms can usually be purchased from September to December. In California, they can be found as late as February. Dried White Matsutake are available year-round.

CULINARY ASPECTS: Wild.

This mushroom is characterized by its unique and unforgettable fragrance, which is both spicy and sweet. Its flavor is similarly energetic, being sufficiently robust to use with game and other strongly flavored meats. It is an all-purpose mushroom that can be used interchangeably in most recipes calling for other mushrooms. Because of its size and firmness, slices can be marinated and then roasted, grilled, or panfried. It is excellent in soups and stir-fry recipes, with grains, and with most meats and fish. Both cap and stem are edible.

Opposite:
Marinating White Matsutakes and fresh as found in nature (*above*).

White Matsutakes are simple to clean. Use a brush to whisk off forest debris and a sharp knife to trim the stem of unwanted soil. As much as possible, avoid using water for cleaning.

White Matsutakes freeze well and will keep for up to a year. Wrap fresh mushrooms in aluminum foil, or cut into pieces and freeze in containers. They can also be dried; however, dried White Matsutakes tend to have less flavor than frozen ones.

COMMENTS: The Japanese Matsutake is a different species. It is called *Tricholoma matsutake* and was formerly called *Armillaria matsutake*. It is considered scarce in Japan because of overpicking, and there are also reports that the pine forests where it grows are being destroyed by parasitic worms that attack the roots of the trees. Because of the scarcity of the Japanese Matsutake, Japan now imports the White Matsutake from the United States, paying extremely high prices.

Occasionally, one can purchase dried Japanese Matsutake. It is the White Matsutake, however, that has gained in popularity recently and is treasured by so many. This popularity has created an increase in the number of commercial mushroom pickers in the Pacific Northwest and may well be considered a threat to our own resource.

Baked Tuna with White Matsutake and Honey-Mustard Sauce

Preheat oven to 350°F.

Place tuna steaks in a baking dish. Combine remaining ingredients, mix well, and pour over tuna. Bake covered for 30 minutes. Remove cover and broil briefly until mushrooms are golden brown.

Serves 4.

Other mushroom choices: Shiitake, White Button, Oyster, Wine-cap Stropharia.

1½ pounds tuna steaks (salmon or halibut may be substituted)
1 tablespoon olive oil
4 cloves garlic, minced
1 cup water
1 teaspoon chicken or vegetable bouillon granules (1 cube)
3 tablespoons Dijon-style prepared mustard
1 tablespoon honey
1 teaspoon dried basil
1 tablespoon minced fresh parsley
Juice of 1 lemon
1 cup sliced White Matsutake

Grilled Flank Steak with White Matsutake

3 cloves garlic, minced
3 tablespoons soy sauce
3 tablespoons vegetable oil
3 tablespoons plum sauce
½ teaspoon grated fresh ginger
  root
1 or 2 dashes hot pepper sauce
¾ cup orange juice
1½ pounds flank steak
1 large White Matsutake (about
  6 ounces), sliced ½ inch thick

Twenty-four hours ahead, combine all ingredients, except steak and mushrooms, in a glass baking dish. Add steak, turning to cover with marinade; cover with plastic wrap and refrigerate overnight, turning steak once or twice.

Ten minutes prior to cooking, remove steak from marinade; add mushrooms, turning to coat well with marinade; and allow to stand 10 minutes. Heat grill. Cook steak as well done as desired, but approximately 5–7 minutes each side, over medium-high heat. Grill mushrooms over medium heat approximately 2 minutes per side or until golden brown.

Serves 4.

Other mushroom choices: Shiitake, Wine-cap Stropharia, King Bolete.

Marinated White Matsutake Salad

Combine first four ingredients in a glass or stainless steel container. Add mushrooms, mixing to coat well. Cover and marinate 10 minutes. Heat grill to medium-high and grill mushrooms until golden brown on each side, or broil in oven until golden brown on both sides. Arrange cooked mushrooms, still warm, on beds of lettuce and garnish as desired with additional vegetables. Use remaining marinade as salad dressing.

Serves 2.

Other mushroom choices: Wine-cap Stropharia, King Bolete, Shiitake.

½ cup balsamic vinegar
¼ cup vegetable oil
1 teaspoon balsam fir needles, ground in mortar and pestle
1 teaspoon sugar
1 large White Matsutake (about 6 ounces), sliced ½ inch thick

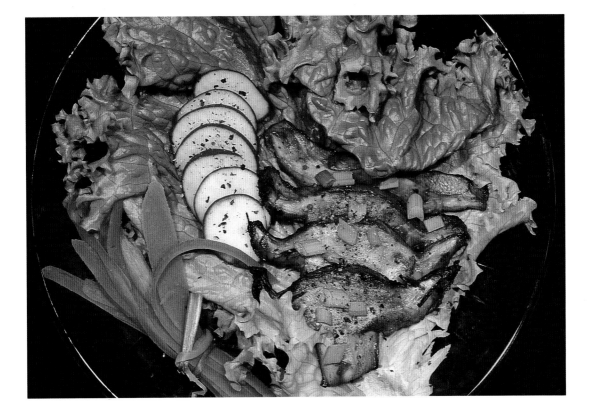

Scallops and White Matsutake with Fennel

1 bulb fresh fennel (sweet anise)
1 cup chicken broth
1 cup coarsely chopped White
  Matsutake
2 tablespoons flour
2 tablespoons butter, softened
1 pound fresh scallops
¼ cup dry white wine

Cut fennel into 2-inch pieces, and place in a large saucepan or skillet with chicken broth and mushrooms. Bring to a boil. Reduce heat, cover, and simmer until fennel is nearly tender (about 15 minutes). Mix flour with butter; add to pan, mixing constantly until sauce is thickened. Add scallops and wine and simmer until scallops are done (about 5 minutes). Season with salt and pepper.

This is a very rich dish and does well with sweet vegetables, such as carrots, on the side. Brown rice is also a nice accompaniment.

Serves 4.

Other mushroom choices: White Button, Oyster, Shiitake, Morel.

Taco-flavored Potatoes and Mushrooms

Preheat oven to 350°F.

Combine first 4 ingredients in a 2-quart baking dish. In a saucepan, heat milk and butter until butter melts; stir in taco seasoning. Pour over potato-mushroom mixture.

Bake, uncovered, for about 45 minutes or until potatoes are tender.

Serves 4–6.

Other mushroom choices: Shiitake, White Button, Wine-cap Stropharia.

1 cup White Matsutake, sliced ¼-inch thick
4 medium potatoes, peeled and sliced ¼-inch thick
1 medium onion, chopped
½ cup chopped bell pepper
1 cup milk
4 tablespoons butter
1–2 tablespoons taco seasoning

Photo shows alternate mushroom choice.

Black Truffle

Tuber melanosporum

OTHER NAMES: French Truffle, Perigord Truffle.

DESCRIPTION: The Black Truffle is an irregularly rounded mushroom that measures ¾–3 inches in diameter. It has a roughened surface consisting of multisided brownish black to black warts. It lacks a stem. Cutting the mushroom in half reveals grayish white flesh that becomes reddish brown and dark brown with white marbling at maturity. The flesh has an agreeable pungent and provocative odor. It grows underground near oaks and other hardwood trees.

HOW SOLD: Fresh, canned, peeled and unpeeled, as peelings alone, and as an extract.

MARKET AVAILABILITY: Seasonal and regional in specialty food shops, typically December through March but sometimes September through May.

CULINARY ASPECTS: Wild.

Truffles, without doubt, are the most highly prized of all mushrooms. This may be because of their characteristically indefinable flavor and aroma or because the demand for them always seems to exceed the supply. Whatever the reason, expect to pay from $200 to $400 per pound for select fresh Truffles. Make certain those you buy are firm, without soft spots. Softness indicates decay. They are excellent eaten raw or cooked. Scrape, sliver, or shave them into egg dishes, sauces of cheese or cream, pasta, and rice. They complement chicken and veal dishes very well. The whole Truffle is edible, including the outer "skin." Its flavor and aroma are so intimately connected that it is difficult to separate one from the other. Eating Truffles is a multisensory experience that combines pungent aromas with elusive flavors. They must be tasted to be understood.

The Black Truffle should be cleaned carefully and thoroughly. A stiff brush and small amounts of water help remove debris. If you decide to peel it after cleaning, make certain to save the peelings for future use. They can be stored submerged in a mild oil or in alcohol (such as vodka) in an airtight container in your refrigerator. Whole Truffles may also be stored this way. Another traditional method of storing fresh Truffles is to bury them in rice grains and keep in a cool location. Truffles, if truly fresh, will impart their aroma and flavor to the rice for you to enjoy after you have used them and later cook the rice. Truffles will also impart their flavor to eggs if wrapped with them and stored in an airtight container in the refrigerator. Truffles should be used as soon after purchase as possible because they lose their flavor and aroma as they age.

COMMENTS: Called the Black Diamond, the Black Truffle is harvested in France. The White Truffle (*Tuber magnatum*) comes from

Italy. While similar to the Black Truffle, the White Truffle has a much stronger aroma. There are also species of Truffles found in Texas, California, and Oregon. These are not considered to be as fine as the European species.

Truffles were eaten by Babylonian nobility. They were enjoyed by the Romans, who believed that Truffles were created by the interaction between thunder and the soil during thunderstorms. The use of pigs to hunt for Truffles was recorded by the Romans. Truffles contain a chemical similar to that which acts as a sex attractant for pigs, which is why pigs are so successful in finding them. Unfortunately, they eat those they find, whenever possible. Dogs have replaced pigs as Truffle scouts, because they are more easily trained not to consume them.

Much has been attributed to Truffles. Perhaps the most intriguing reputed quality is that of being an aphrodisiac. There are stories blaming Truffles for the loosening of morals of otherwise proper young women and men. It might be wise to consider carefully with whom you choose to eat Truffles!

Fresh Black Truffles.

DA

Black Truffle and Cheese Omelet

3 large eggs
½ teaspoon salt
⅛ teaspoon white pepper
1 tablespoon cream or milk
1 tablespoon butter
½ cup grated Cheddar cheese
  (or cheese of your choice)
2–3 teaspoons grated canned
  Black Truffle
Minced green onion for garnish

Combine eggs, salt, white pepper, and cream. Whisk together until slightly frothy. Melt butter in a 10-inch skillet. Add eggs all at once. Spread eggs and move pan in a circular motion until eggs begin to set. When eggs are lightly set (omelet will still be somewhat soft) sprinkle with grated cheese and almost all grated Black Truffle. Fold omelet in half, and garnish with green onions and reserved grated Black Truffle. Serve immediately.

Serves 1–2.

Other mushroom choices: Chanterelle, Morel.

Easy Truffle Cheese Spread

In a small bowl, combine cream cheese and sour cream; blend well. Mix in remaining ingredients. Season to taste with salt and white pepper. Refrigerate 1 hour or more to allow flavors to blend.

Serve on rye toast points, crackers, or raw vegetables.

Makes approximately 1 cup.

1 8-ounce package cream cheese, softened
2 tablespoons sour cream
1 tablespoon minced fresh parsley
1–2 teaspoons grated canned Black Truffle
Ground white pepper

Shrimp and Black Truffle Bisque

¾ **pound raw unshelled shrimp**
1 bay leaf
½ cup water
1 tablespoon grated onion
1 clove garlic, minced
3 tablespoons butter
½ teaspoon salt
¼ teaspoon white pepper
1 tablespoon condensed tomato
   soup
2 tablespoons sherry
1½ cups cream
2 teaspoons grated canned
   Black Truffle

Place shrimp, bay leaf, and water in a saucepan. Bring to a boil. Reduce heat, cover, and simmer 10 minutes. Drain shrimp, reserving liquid. Discard bay leaf. Shell shrimp and puree them with their cooking liquid in a blender or food processor. Set aside.

Sauté onion and garlic in butter until translucent. *Do not brown*. Stir in pureed shrimp, salt, pepper, condensed tomato soup, sherry, and cream. Heat thoroughly without boiling. Serve immediately with grated truffles sprinkled on top.

Serves 2 as main dish, 4 as appetizer.

Truffle Butter

Sauté shallots in 2 tablespoons of the butter until translucent. In small bowl, cream truffles and sautéed shallots into remaining butter, blending well. Let stand, covered, in a cool place for 1 hour to allow flavors to ripen. Chill slightly and shape into a log. Wrap in waxed paper and store in refrigerator. May also be frozen.

Serve with croissants, vegetables, poultry, or other food that is complemented with flavored butter.

Other mushroom choices: Sautéed Morels, Chanterelles, White Matsutake.

2 tablespoons finely minced shallots
¾ cup butter, softened
1–2 teaspoons grated canned Black Truffles

OTHER NAMES: Rough Ring, King Stropharia, Giant Stropharia.

DESCRIPTION: The cap is typically 2–6 inches wide and umbrella shaped, but may attain a diameter of more than one foot when cultivated. The edge is incurved when young but nearly flat when old. It is purple-red to reddish brown and fades to pale yellowish brown at maturity. It is dry and often cracked. The stem is 3–6 inches long, enlarged toward the base, and is attached to the center of the cap. It is thick and white and supports a thick, white, scaly, membranous ring. Gills are found on the undersurface of the cap. They are white on very young specimens and are covered by a narrow band of white tissue. The gills become purple-black with age. The cap and stem flesh is thick, firm, and white. It grows singly or in groups on wood chips.

HOW SOLD: Fresh.

MARKET AVAILABILITY: Sporadic.

CULINARY ASPECTS: Cultivated and wild.

This hardy and robust mushroom really earns its name of *Giant*. It is not unusual to find individual mushrooms that weigh several pounds. The entire mushroom is edible, with a firm and somewhat crisp texture. Its flavor is reminiscent of raw potatoes. Because of its size and firm flesh, it broils, grills, and bakes well. It can be marinated and basted prior to cooking. Its unique flavor is nicely complemented by sour cream, dill, bacon, horseradish, and caraway.

The Wine-cap Stropharia is easily cleaned with a brush or cloth. Since it grows primarily in wood chips, there is usually little debris associated with it. It can be stored in the refrigerator for about a week. It freezes well after blanching or sautéing and also pickles well. We do not recommend drying it.

COMMENTS: The Wine-cap Stropharia might be considered the New Wave of tamed wild mushrooms. It is cultivated on a limited basis in Europe and North America. Experimentation with commercial cultivation is under way. This mushroom is relatively easy to grow, tolerating a wide range of temperatures. In terms of market availability, we believe it may be the mushroom of the future.

Wine-cap Stropharia

Stropharia rugosoannulata

Opposite:
A field photograph of fresh Wine-cap Stropharias growing in their natural habitat.

Baked Salmon with Crab and Mushroom Stuffing

2 cups finely chopped Wine-cap
  Stropharia
½ cup minced onion
2 cloves garlic, minced
¼ cup finely chopped bell
  pepper
½ stick (¼ cup) butter
8 ounces crabmeat or crabmeat
  substitute (about 1 cup)
1 egg, lightly beaten
¼ cup white wine
½ teaspoon salt
¼ teaspoon black pepper
⅛ teaspoon cayenne pepper
¼–½ cup cracker meal (more
  or less, as needed)
Fresh whole salmon, 4–5
  pounds
Vegetable oil

Sauté mushrooms, onion, garlic, and bell pepper in butter until onion is translucent. Mix in all remaining ingredients except salmon and vegetable oil, adding enough cracker meal to absorb excess liquid. Stuff salmon with this mixture and sew shut with string or unwaxed dental floss.

Preheat oven to 350°F.

Brush salmon with oil or melted butter to prevent drying. Place in baking dish and cover with aluminum foil. Bake covered for 1 hour. Uncover and bake an additional 30 minutes until lightly browned and easily flaked with a fork.

Serves 6–8.

Other mushroom choices: Shiitake, White Matsutake, White Button, Oyster.

Mushroom Scampi

Cut mushrooms into ½-inch slices. If small, quarter them instead. Melt butter in a large skillet. Add mushrooms and garlic and sauté over medium heat about 10 minutes (until juices are released). Add parsley, lemon juice, wine, and clam juice. Add seasonings (crushed red pepper flakes and salt and pepper) to taste and heat until bubbly hot. Serve over linguine cooked al dente.

Makes 4 servings.

Other mushroom choices: White Button, King Bolete, Shiitake.

1 pound Wine-cap Stropharias
4 tablespoons butter
3 large cloves garlic, minced
¼ cup chopped fresh parsley
   (1 tablespoon dried)
1 tablespoon fresh lemon juice
¼ cup dry white wine
½ cup clam juice
Pinch crushed red pepper flakes
   (optional)
Linguine

Photo shows alternate mushroom choice.

Turkey-Mushroom Casserole

3 tablespoons butter
4 tablespoons flour
1 13- to 15-ounce can chicken
  broth
¼ cup dry vermouth
2 teaspoons dried basil
1 teaspoon garlic salt
½ teaspoon black pepper
8 ounces Wine-cap Stropharias,
  sliced ½-inch thick
1 cup chopped celery
1 cup chopped onion
1 cup sliced carrots (¼-inch
  rounds)
½ cup chopped roasted sweet
  red peppers
2 cups (about ½ pound)
  uncooked turkey, cut into
  1-inch pieces

Preheat oven to 375°F.

Melt butter in a saucepan; mix in flour and cook over medium heat about 3 minutes. Slowly whisk in chicken broth; cook until thickened. Add vermouth, basil, garlic salt, and pepper. Combine remaining ingredients in a buttered 2- to 2½-quart baking dish. Add sauce, mixing to blend.

Bake 30 minutes covered; mix and bake another 30 minutes uncovered. Serves 4–6.

Other mushroom choices: White Button, Shiitake, Chanterelle, Oyster.

Photo shows alternate mushroom choice.

Vegetable Fusilli with Cheese Sauce

Sauté garlic and onion in olive oil over medium-high heat until softened. Add broccoflower and stir-fry 3 minutes. Add mushrooms and cook 2–3 minutes more. Add kidney beans, mix well, and heat through.

Cook fusilli according to package directions (about 15 minutes).

Using a food processor or blender, puree cottage cheese with Parmesan cheese, basil, and pepper flakes. Drain pasta. Add cheese mixture and vegetables, mixing to blend.

Serves 4.

Other mushroom choices: Morel, Chanterelle, White Button, Paddy Straw, King Bolete.

4 cloves garlic, minced
1 cup coarsely chopped onion
2 tablespoons olive oil
2 cups broccoflower (or broccoli or cauliflower) flowerets
2 cups Wine-cap Stropharia, sliced ½-inch thick
1 cup canned kidney beans, drained
8 ounces fusilli
16 ounces cottage cheese
¼ cup grated Parmesan cheese
2 teaspoons minced fresh basil (¼ teaspoon dried)
Pinch crushed red pepper flakes

4.

Beyond the Marketplace

MANY PEOPLE who enjoy the bounty of the marketplace become curious about foraging and eating wild mushrooms that are not commercially available. Many wild mushrooms are easy to identify, and with a little training, collecting wild mushrooms for the table can be a safe, enjoyable, and richly rewarding pastime. Information on where to learn about wild mushrooms, including notes on a national organization, local clubs, seminars, and workshops, is provided in this section.

One question often asked is, How can I learn more about wild mushrooms? One of the best ways is to join a local mushroom club. Clubs are located throughout North America and most are affiliated with a national organization called *NAMA:* the North American Mycological Association. A list of the known mycological clubs in North America is presented below (courtesy of NAMA). Information about membership in one of these organizations can be obtained by writing to the club's address.

Other sources of information about wild mushrooms may be obtained by contacting your local cooperative extension service, colleges and universities, botanical gardens, nature centers, and the U.S. Forestry Service.

Workshops and seminars about wild mushroom identification are offered in several states. The authors offer mycological workshops that include instruction on collecting and identifying wild mushrooms, as well as methods for preparation and preservation of edible species. For additional information contact:

Dr. Alan Bessette
Biology Department
Utica College of Syracuse University
1600 Burrstone Road
Utica, NY 13502
315-792-3132

An excellent publication, *Mushroom—The Journal of Wild Mushrooming,* is available by subscription and features articles about mushroom identification, methods of preparation, tips on collecting, anecdotes, book reviews, and many other topics. For subscription information write to:

Mushroom
Box 3156, University Station
Moscow, ID 83843

Opposite:
Golden Oyster Mushroom Patch

Growing Your Own Mushrooms

Growing Mushrooms at home has become a popular and enjoyable pastime in much of North America. Kits are available that contain spawn (live mushroom culture) and all the ingredients required for growth. Instructions for watering and maintaining proper growing conditions (temperature, light or darkness, etc.) accompany each kit. Several species with unusual names and fascinating shapes will excite your senses. Examples include the Monkey's Head (Lion's Mane) Mushroom Patch, the Oyster Mushroom Patch, the Golden Oyster Mushroom Patch, the Enokitake Mushroom Patch, and the Pom Pom Blanc Mushroom Patch. Kits are also available for mushrooms esteemed for their alleged immune-system-stimulating properties. Examples include the Reishi/Ling Zhi Mushroom Patch and the Shiitake Mushroom Patch.

Outdoor home mushroom cultivation is also increasing in popularity and several kinds are available. Some are grown in lawns, others on logs and stumps, and a few in a mixture of wood chips and sawdust. Examples include the Lion's Mane Mushroom, Chicken of the Woods, the Cauliflower Mushroom, the Shaggy Mane, and the King Stropharia Mushroom Patches.

Those who wish to learn about mushroom cultivation using a hands-on approach can register for workshops held at Fungi Perfecti in Olympia, Washington. Five basic workshops, one advanced program, and a master's course are offered annually. They are taught by Paul Stamets, an international authority on mushroom cultivation.

Paul Stamets and Jeff Childon have coauthored *The Mushroom Cultivator,* a practical guide to growing mushrooms at home. This is a widely used reference book that many have called the bible of mushroom cultivation. Another valuable resource, *Growing Gourmet Mushrooms,* is also available. For additional information about mushroom cultivation workshops and cultivation equipment, books, and supplies, contact Fungi Perfecti.

The following is a list of names, addresses and telephone numbers of companies that sell mushroom kits. They offer catalogues and other information about growing mushrooms at home.

Far West Fungi
P.O. Box 428
South San Francisco, CA 94083
415-871-0786

Gourmet Mushrooms, Inc.
P.O. Box 515
Graton, CA 95444
707-823-1743

Fungi Perfecti
P.O. Box 7634
Olympia, WA 98507
206-426-9292

Mushroompeople
P.O. Box 220/The Farm
Summertown, TN 38483
615-964-2200

Specialty Food Suppliers

The following is a list of names, addresses, and phone numbers of specialty food suppliers that sell common and exotic mushrooms.

American Spoon Foods
P.O. Box 566
Petoskey, MI 49770
800-222-5886

Epicurean Specialty
Dept. 486
P.O. Box 597004
San Francisco, CA 94159

Fungi Perfecti
P.O. Box 7634
Olympia, WA 98507
206-426-9292

Gourmet Mushrooms, Inc.
P.O. Box 515
Graton, CA 95444
707-823-1743

Kirsch Mushroom Co., Inc.
751 Drake St.
Bronx, NY 10474
212-991-4977

La Cuisine
323 Cameron St.
Alexandria, VA 22314
703-836-4435
800-521-1176

Majestic Morels
No. 2 P.J.'s Place
Hendersonville, NC 28792
704-684-6267

Phillips Mushroom Place
909 E. Baltimore Pike
Kennett Square, PA 19348
215-388-6082

Specialty World Foods
84 Montgomery St.
Albany, NY 12207
518-436-7603
800-233-0193

Todaro Brothers
555 Second Ave.
New York, NY 10016
212-679-7766

Williams-Sonoma
Mail Order Department
P.O. Box 7456
San Francisco, CA 94120
800-541-2233

Mycological Clubs of North America *Arranged in alphabetical order by state*

Glacier Bay Mycological Society, P.O. Box 65, Gustavus, AK 99826-0065
Alaska Mycological Society, P.O. Box 2526, Homer, AK 99603-2526

Arkansas Mycological Society, 5115 S. Main St., Pine Bluff, AR 71601-7452

Humboldt Bay Mycological Society, P.O. Box 4419, Arcata, CA 95521-1419
Los Angeles Mycological Society, Biology, 5151 State University Dr., Los Angeles, CA 90032
Mount Shasta Mycological Society, 623 Pony Trail, Mount Shasta, CA 96067-9769
Mycological Society of San Francisco, 219 Sequoia Ave., Redwood City, CA 94061-3424
Fungus Federation of Santa Cruz, 1305 E. Cliff Dr. (Museum), Santa Cruz, CA 95062-3722

Pikes Peak Mycological Society, P.O. Box 1961, Colorado Springs, CO 80901-1961
Colorado Mycological Society, P.O. Box 9621, Denver, CO 80209-0621

Connecticut Valley Mycological Society, 21 Johnson St., Naugatuck, CT 06770-4214
Nutmeg Mycological Society, 191 Mile Creek Rd., % Kovak, Old Lyme, CT 06371-1719

Mycological Association of Washington, 2327 49th St. NW, Washington, DC 20007-1002

Prairie States Mushroom Club, 310 Central Dr., Pella, IA 50219-1901

Southern Idaho Mycological Association, P.O. Box 843, Boise, ID 83701-0843
North Idaho Mycological Association, 5936 N. Mount Carrol St., Coeur d'Alene, ID 83814-9609

Illinois Mycological Association, 562 Iroquois Trail, % Serra, Carol Stream, IL 60188

Kaw Valley Mycological Society, 601 Mississippi St., Lawrence, KS 66044-2349

Gulf States Mycological Society, 1000 Adams St., New Orleans, LA 70118-3540

Boston Mycological Club, 100 Memorial Dr., % Hrbek, Cambridge, MA 02142-1314
Berkshire Mycological Society, Pleasant Valley Sanctuary, Lenox, MA 01240

Lower East Shore Mushroom Club, R.R. 1, Box 94B, Princess Anne, MD 21853-9801

Maine Mycological Association, Love's Cove, % Bannister, West Southport, ME 04576

Albion Mushroom Club, Whitehouse Nature Center, Albion, MI 49224
North American Mycological Association, 3556 Oakwood St., Ann Arbor, MI 48104-5213
Michigan Mushroom Hunters Club, 23209 Haynes St., % Stevenson, Farmington Hills, MI 48336-3340
Lewiston Fun Country Mushroom Hunters Club, P.O. Box 783, Lewiston, MI 49756-0783
West Michigan Mycological Society, 923 E. Ludington Ave., Ludington, MI 49431-2437

Minnesota Mycological Society, 7637 E. River Rd., Fridley, MN 55432-3058

Missouri Mycological Society, 2888 Ossenfort Rd., Glencoe, MO 63038-1716

Asheville Mushroom Club, Nature Center, Gashes Creek Rd., Asheville, NC 28805
Triangle Area Mushroom Club, P.O. Box 61061, Durham, NC 27705-1061
Blue Ridge Mushroom Club, P.O. Box 2032, North Wilkesboro, NC 28659-2032
Cape Fear Mycological Society, % Dickman, 10 Scots Hill Rd., Wilmington, NC 28405

Monadnock Mushroomers Unlimited, P.O. Box 6296, Keene, NH 03431-6296
New Hampshire Mycological Society, 84 Cannongate III, Nashua, NH 03063-1948

Montshire Mycological Club, P.O. Box 59, % Carlson, Sunapee, NH 03782-0059

New Jersey Mycological Association, 20 Lorraine Terr., Boonton, NJ 07005-1240

New Mexico Mycological Society, 1511 Marble Ave. NW, Albuquerque, NM 87104-1347

Long Island Mycological Club, 231-04 64th Ave., Flushing, NY 11364-2417
Mid Hudson Mycological Association, 43 South St., Highland, NY 12528-2418
COMA, % Sheine, R.R. 3, Box 137B, Pound Ridge, NY 10576-9803
New York Mycological Society, 140 W. 13th St., % Williams, New York, NY 10011-7802
Rochester Area Mycological Association, 711 Corwin Rd., % Rains, Rochester, NY 14610-2124
Mid York Mycological Society, 2995 Mohawk St., % Smith, Sauquoit, NY 13456
Central New York Mycological Society, 343 Randolph St., Syracuse, NY 13205-2357

Ohio Mushroom Society, 288 E. North Ave., East Palestine, OH 44413-2369

North American Truffling Society, P.O. Box 296, Corvallis, OR 97339-0296
Oregon Coast Mycological Society, P.O. Box 1590, Florence, OR 97439-0103
Mount Mazama Mushroom Association, 417 Garfield St., Medford, OR 97501-4028
Lincoln County Mycological Society, P.O. Box 1105, Newport, OR 97365
Oregon Mycological Society, 2781 S.W. Sherwood Dr., Portland, OR 97201-2250
Pacific Northwest Key Council, 1943 S.E. Locust Ave., Portland, OR 97214-4826
Willamette Valley Mushroom Society, 2610 E. Nob Hill St. SE, Salem, OR 97302-4429

Texas Mycological Society, 7445 Dillon, Houston, TX 77061-2721

Montshire Mycological Club, R.D. #1, Box 336, Windsor, VT 05089

Northwest Mushroomers Association, 831 Mason St., % Marlowe, Bellingham, WA 98225-5715
Kitsap Peninsula Mycological Society, P.O. Box 265, Bremerton, WA 98310-0054
Wenatchee Valley Mushroom Society, 287 N. Iowa Ave., East Wenatchee, WA 98802-5205
Snohomish County Mycological Society, P.O. Box 2822, Everett, WA 98203-0822
Olympic Mountain Mycological Society, P.O. Box 720, Forks, WA 98331-0720
South Sound Mushroom Club, 6439 32nd Ave. NW, Olympia, WA 98502-9519
Puget Sound Mycological Society, U. of W. Urban Hort. #GF-15, Seattle, WA 98195-0001
Spokane Mushroom Club, P.O. Box 2791, Spokane, WA 99220-2791
Tacoma Mushroom Society, P.O. Box 99577, Tacoma, WA 98499-0577

Northwestern Wisconsin Mycological Society, R.R. 03, Box 17, Frederic, WI 54837-9803
Parkside Mycological Club, 5219 85th St., Kenosha, WI 53142-3209
Wisconsin Mycological Society, Room 614, M.P.M., 800 W. Wells, Milwaukee, WI 53233-1404

Le Cercle Sporée Boréal, 804 5e Rue, Chibougamau, PQ Canada G8P 1V4
Cercle des Mycologues du Saguenay, 438 Rue Perrault, Chicoutimi, PQ Canada G7J 3Y9
Cercle des Mycologues de Montreal, 4101 Rue Sherbrooke Est., 125, Montreal, PQ Canada H1X 2B2
Cercle des Mycologues de Rimouski, Univ. of Quebec, Rimouski, Rimouski, PQ Canada
Cercle Mycologues de Quebec, Pav. Comtois, Univ. Laval, Sainte-Foy, PQ Canada G1K 7P4

Mycological Society of Toronto, 2 Deepwood Crescent, North York, ONT Canada M3C 1N8

Edmonton Mycological Club, % Schmidt, 6003 109 B Ave., Edmonton, ALTA Canada T6A 1S7

Vancouver Mycological Society, 403 Third St., New Westminster, BC Canada V31 2S1

Butter: 1 stick = ½ cup = 8 tablespoons
Celery: 3 stalks = 1 cup diced
Cheese, shredded: ¼ pound = 1 cup
Garlic: 1 small clove = ⅛ teaspoon powder
Ginger, fresh: 1 tablespoon grated = ⅛ teaspoon powdered
Green pepper: 1 large (6 ounces) = 1 cup diced
Herbs, fresh: 1 tablespoon fresh = ⅓–½ teaspoon dried
Lemon: 1 medium lemon = 3 tablespoons juice
Mushrooms, canned: 6 ounces drained = 8 ounces fresh
Mushrooms, dried: 3 ounces dried = 1 pound fresh
Mushrooms, fresh: 8 ounces = 3 cups sliced raw = 1 cup sliced cooked
Onion: 1 large onion = ¾–1 cup chopped
Spaghetti: 1 pound dry = 5–6 cups cooked
Tomato: 3 medium tomatoes = approximately 1 pound

APPENDIX A.
Equivalents and Substitutions for Common Ingredients

VOLUME

1 Quart	=	32 ounces	=	0.95 liter
1 Cup	=	8 ounces	=	237 milliliters
½ Cup	=	4 ounces	=	118 milliliters
⅓ Cup	=	2.7 ounces	=	79 milliliters
¼ Cup	=	2 ounces	=	59 milliliters
⅛ Cup	=	1 ounce	=	30 milliliters
1 Tablespoon	=	½ ounce	=	15 milliliters
1 Teaspoon	=	⅙ ounce	=	5 milliliters
½ Teaspoon	=	1/12 ounce	=	2.5 milliliters
¼ Teaspoon	=	1/24 ounce	=	1.25 milliliters

APPENDIX B.
Conversion Tables

WEIGHT

1 Pound	=	16 ounces	=	454 grams
½ Pound	=	8 ounces	=	227 grams
¼ Pound	=	4 ounces	=	114 grams
⅛ Pound	=	2 ounces	=	57 grams
1/16 Pound	=	1 ounce	=	28 grams
1/32 Pound	=	½ ounce	=	14 grams

TEMPERATURE

Very low oven	250°F–275°F	=	121°C–133°C
Low oven	300°F–325°F	=	149°C–163°C
Moderate oven	350°F–375°F	=	177°C–190°C
Hot oven	400°F–425°F	=	204°C–218°C
Very hot oven	450°F–475°F	=	232°C–246°C

Recommended Reading

Arora, David. *All That the Rain Promises, and More . . . : A Hip Pocket Guide to Western Mushrooms*. Berkeley, Calif.: Ten Speed Press, 1991.

———. *Mushrooms Demystified: A Comprehensive Guide to the Fleshy Fungi*. 2d ed. Berkeley, Calif.: Ten Speed Press, 1986.

Bessette, Alan E. *Guide to Some Edible and Poisonous Mushrooms of New York*. Rome, N.Y.: Canterbury Press, 1985.

———. *Mushrooms of the Adirondacks: A Field Guide*. Utica, N.Y.: North Country Books, 1988.

Bessette, Alan, and Walter J. Sundberg. *Mushrooms: A Quick Reference Guide to Mushrooms of North America*. New York: Macmillan, 1987.

Brodie, Harold J. *Fungi: Delight of Curiosity*. Toronto: University of Toronto Press, 1978.

Carluccio, Antonio. *A Passion for Mushrooms*. Topsfield, Mass.: Salem House, 1989.

Cazort, Mimi, ed. *Mr. Jackson's Mushrooms*. Toronto: National Museum of Canada, 1979.

Czarnecki, Jack. *Joe's Book of Mushroom Cookery*. New York: Atheneum, 1986.

Dickinson, C., and J. Lucas. *The Encyclopedia of Mushrooms*. New York: Putnam, 1979.

Findlay, W. P. K. *Fungi: Folklore, Fiction and Fact*. Richmond, England: Richmond Publishing, 1982.

Fischer, David W., and Alan E. Bessette. *Edible Wild Mushrooms of North America: A Field-to-Kitchen Guide*. Austin: University of Texas Press, 1992.

Freedman, Louise. *Wild about Mushrooms: A Cookbook for Feasters and Foragers*. Berkeley, Calif.: Aris Books, 1987.

Friedman, Sara Ann. *Celebrating the Wild Mushroom: A Passionate Quest*. New York: Dodd, Mead & Co., 1986.

Harris, Robert. *Growing Wild Mushrooms*. Berkeley, Calif.: Wingbow Press, 1976.

Huffman, Don M., Lois H. Tiffany, and George Knaphus. *Mushrooms and Other Fungi of the Midcontinental United States*. Ames: Iowa State University Press, 1989.

Leibenstein, Margaret. *The Edible Mushroom: A Gourmet Cook's Guide*. New York: Ballantine Books, 1986.

Lincoff, Gary H. *The Audubon Society Field Guide to North American Mushrooms*. New York: Knopf, 1981.

McKenny, Margaret, and Daniel E. Stuntz. *The New Savory Wild Mushroom*. Revised and enlarged by Joseph F. Ammirati. Seattle: University of Washington Press, 1987.

McKnight, Kent H., and Vera B. McKnight. *A Field Guide to Mushrooms of North America*. Boston: Houghton Mifflin, 1987.

Marteka, Vincent. *Mushrooms: Wild and Edible*. New York: Norton, 1980.

Metzler, Susan, and Van Metzler. *Texas Mushrooms: A Field Guide*. Scientific advisor, Orson K. Miller, Jr. Austin: University of Texas Press, 1992.

Miller, Orson K., Jr. *Mushrooms of North America*. New York: Dutton, 1979.

Miller, Orson K., Jr., and Hope H. Miller. *Mushrooms in Color*. New York: Dutton, 1980.

Phillips, Roger. *Mushrooms of North America*. Boston: Little, Brown, 1991.

Riedlinger, Thomas J., ed. *The Sacred Mushroom Seeker: Essays for R. Gordon Wasson*. Portland, Ore.: Dioscorides Press, 1990.

Smith, Alexander H. *A Field Guide to Western Mushrooms*. Ann Arbor: University of Michigan Press, 1975.

Smith, Alexander H., and Nancy S. Weber. *The Mushroom Hunter's Field Guide*. Ann Arbor: University of Michigan Press, 1980.

Stamets, Paul, and Jeff S. Chilton. *The Mushroom Cultivator*. Olympia, Wash.: Agarikon Press, 1983.

States, Jack S. *Mushrooms and Truffles of the Southwest*. Tucson: University of Arizona Press, 1990.

Tylutki, Edmond E. *Mushrooms of Idaho and the Pacific Northwest*. Vol. 2, *Non-gilled Hymenomycetes*. Moscow: University of Idaho Press, 1987.

Wasson, R. Gordon, with Wendy Doniger O'Flaherty. *Soma: Divine Mushroom of Immortality*. New York: Harcourt Brace Jovanovich, 1968.

Weber, Nancy S. *A Morel Hunter's Companion*. Lansing, Mich.: Two Peninsula Press, 1988.

Weber, Nancy S., and Alexander H. Smith. *A Field Guide to Southern Mushrooms*. Ann Arbor: University of Michigan Press, 1985.

Ying, J., X. Mao, Q. Ma, Y. Zong, and H. Wen. *Icons of Medicinal Fungi from China*. Beijing: Science Press, 1987.

Index Boldfaced page numbers refer to photographs.